PARTY TO MURDER

A Thriller

OLIVE CHASE and STEWART BURKE

SAMUEL FRENCH

LONDON

NEW YORK TORONTO SYDNEY HOLLYWOOD

PARTY TO MURDER

First tour presented by Knightsbridge Productions at the Theatre Royal, Windsor, on 2nd November 1971, with the following cast of characters:

Ray Lewis	Paul Greenwood
Sheila Hilton	Diane Keen
Tony Marshall	Michael Malnick
Norma Brent	Helen Cherry
Stephen Brent, M.A.	David Knight
Cliff Prior	Marshall Jones
Joan Prior	Joyce Donaldson
Diane Winslow	Helen Cherry

The play directed by Joan Riley

Subsequent tour presented by David Gordon Productions at The Ashcroft Theatre, Croydon, on the 24th September 1973, with the following cast of characters:

Ray Lewis	Ian Kellgren
Sheila Hilton	Nadine Hanwell
Tony Marshall	James Greene
Norma Brent	Ros Drinkwater
Stephen Brent, M.A.	Ty Hardin
Joan Prior	Patricia Driscoll
Cliff Prior	Murray Brown
Diane Winslow	Ros Drinkwater

The play directed by Kim Grant

NOTE: The roles of Norma and Diane should be doubled by the same actress, wearing a blonde wig in Act I

The action takes place in the Lounge Hall of Tudor Gables, the home of Professor Stephen Brent and his wife, Norma, in a new university town

ACT I
    Scene 1   10 p.m., a Tuesday in October
    Scene 2   9.15 a.m., Wednesday
    Scene 3   Early evening, one week later

ACT II
    Scene 1   Four hours later
    Scene 2   Midnight, the following night
    Scene 3   Fifteen minutes later
    Scene 4   The next evening

Time – the present

ACT I

Scene 1

The Lounge Hall of Tudor Gables, home of Professor Stephen Brent and his wife Norma, in a new university town. Tuesday, 10 p.m.

The half-timbered, beamed room has twin archways at the back, one leading to the hall, where there is an unseen coat closet and front door, the other to the dining-room and kitchen. Between them is a high bookcase set in an alcove. A staircase rises to a gallery half-way up. Diamond-paned windows flank a Tudor fireplace, which has an electric log fire in the grate. Down stage a curtained garden door leads to the patio

When the Curtain *rises, the hall is illuminated by moonlight from the windows and garden door. There is the sound of rain, muted*

Ray and Sheila appear, like shadows, outside the garden door, which he forces with a celluloid plectrum. He enters, wearing a shiny, wet-looking windcheater, hooded, and switches on the lights by the garden door. He goes into the middle of the room and beckons to Sheila, who is hovering timidly on the threshold. She wears a trendy jacket with large buttons, over a sweater and slacks. Ray, a student nephew of Norma, is a brash boy of twenty. Sheila Hilton, his pretty, trendy girl-friend is eighteen

Ray Come on, what's the hang up?

Sheila I feel like a burglar.

Ray (*amused*) For God's sake . . . shut the door, the rain's coming in.

He kicks on the electric fire, while she closes the door

Sheila (*coming into the middle of the room*) Well?

Ray What?

Sheila Go on, tell your aunt we're here.

Ray She's out.

Sheila You can't be certain.

Ray She must be. I banged on the front door loud enough to wake the dead.

Sheila Make sure.

Ray If you insist. (*Calling at the dining-room archway*) Norma—Norma!

Sheila Where does that lead to?

Ray Dining-room and kitchen. See, she's not there.

Sheila She might be upstairs. Having an early night.

Ray If she is, she won't be alone. (*He winks, mounts the stairs*) Norma! Nor-ma. (*Coming down again*) Told you.

Sheila We'd better go, then. She might be mad at us, forcing our way in . . .

Ray But I used to live here.

Sheila Well, you don't live here now. (*Moving round the room*) It's sort of creepy, isn't it?

Ray (*at the wine cabinet*) Drink?

Sheila We shouldn't, Ray . . .

Ray (*examines bottles*) Gin, vodka, Scotch, sherry . . .

Sheila Bitter lemon, please.

Ray What, when it's free? (*He pours drinks*)

Sheila I wouldn't like to live here.

Ray You won't have to.

Sheila I imagined it would be—well, different, modern, as your aunt's stinking rich.

Ray And stinking mean with it.

Sheila How much did she inherit?

Ray Too much.

Sheila (*rubbing her sleeves*) My jacket's wet.

Ray Take it off and dry it, then.

Sheila removes her jacket and drapes it over a chair. Ray takes a drink to her

Sheila You should have stopped and put up the hood. Oh, dear, my hair's damp.

Ray (*touching it*) M'm, so it is. I know: there's a hair dryer in Norma's bedroom. Come on. (*He drags her towards the stairs*)

Sheila That's just an excuse to get me upstairs.

Ray (*pulling her up the stairs*) I only want to get your hair dry.

Sheila No! She'll think the worst if she finds us up there.

Ray She won't be home for ages. Come on, love.

The telephone rings

Ray Oh, hell!

Sheila Well, go on, answer it.

Ray Won't be for me.

Sheila It might be your Uncle Stephen.

Ray What, ringing all the way from New York?

Sheila Why not? Answer it. (*She pushes him*) Go on, Ray.

Ray (*sighing and coming down*) Right, you fetch the dryer, then. You can use it down here.

Sheila Which door?

Ray Second on the right.

Sheila exits upstairs

Ray (*on the phone*) Tudor Gables . . . Oh, hallo, Mrs Prior . . . Sorry, she's out . . . Is he? Fine . . . Yes, I'll tell her when she . . .

There is a knock on the front door

Someone at the door. Have to go. Chow. (*He replaces the receiver*)

Ray exits to the hall, returning with Tony Marshall, a good-looking bachelor in tweeds. He is in his late thirties

Ray No idea when she'll be in.

Tony Well, actually I dropped by because I heard Stephen might be coming back today. Is he home yet?

Ray He's on his way from the airport. Joan Prior next door rang and told me.

Tony Good. I'll wait for him, then.

Sheila appears on the stairs, holding a white hair-dryer aloft, like a torch. She looks at Tony, who moves to the side of the gallery

FRENO IT

Sheila Oh!

Tony Well, well, the Statue of Liberty!

Sheila Hallo, Professor Brent.

Ray This isn't Stephen, it's Tony Marshall. (*To Tony*) My girl friend, Sheila Hilton.

Tony Delighted to meet you, Sheila.

Sheila I was just going to dry my hair. It got damp in the rain.

Tony What a pity. Such lovely hair, too.

Ray (*jealously*) Come on down or the ghost will get you!

Sheila (*scuttling down*) This house isn't haunted, is it?

Ray 'Course. (*He takes the dryer and plugs it into a socket*) All old places are haunted. Didn't you hear weird sounds upstairs? Creaking footsteps, low groans?

Tony (*amused*) Take no notice, he's only teasing you.

Ray hands her the dryer, she clicks on the two small switches, the dryer purrs, and she fans it over her hair

Sheila Isn't this weather dreadful?

Tony Foul. The links deserted, puddles on the fairway.

Ray (*to Sheila*) Tony's secretary of the golf club.

Tony Looks more like a *swimming* club at present. Still, we have our little diversions.

Ray I bet you do.

Tony We're getting up a Christmas show, Norma's cast to play the lead. Did she tell you, Ray?

Ray She tells me damn all. (*Going to the cabinet*) Like a quencher?

Tony I'll have a Scotch. Neat. How are the new digs?

Ray Bit ropey. The old duck won't let me have Sheila in.

Sheila This show you're putting on—is it a panto?

Tony No, we're doing *Lysistrata*.

Sheila Oh, highbrow.

Tony Not really. It's a fascinating play, quite spicy, too. No censorship for the Ancient Greeks.

Ray (*taking a drink to him*) The original permissive society.

Tony Well, you know what they say: "The Greeks had a word for it."

Ray A four-letter word?

Sheila giggles. Tony frowns

Tony I'm hoping Stephen will give me some tips on the production side, as he often directs plays at the university . . .

Ray He'll be tired after his lecture tour. Why not leave it till another day?

Tony Am I in the way, then?

Sheila No, no, of course not, Tony . . . Why didn't your aunt go to America, Ray?

Ray Too busy raving it up at the golf club. All those groovey male swingers. (*He mimes a golf swing*)

Tony What are you hinting?

Ray I thought *you* knew the score. Our Norma doesn't like being lonely, does she?

Tony (*slamming down his empty glass*) Don't talk about her like that.

Ray I was only joking.

Tony No, you weren't. The youth of today—morals of the farmyard yourselves and you think everyone else is . . .

Ray Oh, crap! No sense of humour, that's your handicap!

Tony And no manners, that's yours! Don't they teach you any at your plate-glass university?

Ray They teach us to think for ourselves.

Tony Pity you don't, then.

Ray Oh, sod off!

Sheila Ray!

Tony (*furiously*) My God, you bloody students! Never do a stroke of work, just live off the taxpayer and go on demos!

Ray (*raising a hand*) Down with golf club secretaries!

Tony I won't wait for Stephen now. Ask him to give me a ring. And tell Norma I'll see her on Friday.

Ray Like that, is it?

Tony At rehearsal. Good night, Sheila.

Sheila Good night, Tony.

Tony strides out

Ray Good riddance, pompous old ponce!

Sheila I thought he was rather dishy. Is it true—that your aunt sleeps around?

Ray Her favourite pastime.

Sheila With him?

Ray Wouldn't surprise me. Go on, you're dry.

Ray switches off the dryer at the plug, goes to the typewriter, slips in a paper and types away. Sheila lets the dryer fall, accidentally, off the table. She picks it up, examines it, looks guilty, then replaces it on the table and goes to Ray

Sheila Does your Uncle Stephen know?
Ray Know what?
Sheila That she carries on with other fellas when he's away?
Ray No, he'd blow his mind.
Sheila He's still in love with her, then?
Ray I dunno, I bet they only do it at Christmas!
Sheila (*giggling*) Funny letters, all curly.
Ray Italics. Norma uses this to type love notes to Stephen. (*He removes the paper, throws it in the waste-paper basket*)
Sheila Why love notes to *him*, if she fancies someone else?
Ray It's a cover-up. She used to leave the notes in Plato's *Republic*. (*He finds a note in a book on the desk*) Told you. She's still at it.
Sheila What's it say?
Ray I'm surprised at you. This is private, meant only for Stephen. (*Reading*) "Stephen, darling, welcome home. If I'm in bed when you arrive, wake me up . . ." Dot! dot, dot! (*He winks, and replaces the note*)
Sheila (*laughing*) You've got a randy mind.
Ray (*grabbing her*) Yes, where you're concerned. Come on, you sexy puss.

He waltzes her towards the settee, pulls her down on it and they kiss and cuddle

Sheila We *are* going to get married, aren't we, Ray?
Ray Sure, love, when I can screw some loot out of Norma.
Sheila Why, does *she* control your legacy?
Ray M'm, the old man made her sole trustee. I have to wait five years. Unless she snuffs it first. (*Slowly*) Then I'd collect the lot. No problems (*His love-making becomes more violent*)

Unseen by them, Norma enters from the hall. She is a strikingly attractive blonde in her thirties, in evening dress and wrap. She pauses in the archway, regarding them with cynical amusement, then moves into the room

Norma Good evening.

Ray and Sheila leap up, startled

Ray Oh—er—hallo, Norma. We didn't hear you . . .
Norma How did you get in?
Ray The garden door—it was open.
Norma (*moving to the garden door*) I closed it before I went out. So you must have broken in, Ray.
Ray We couldn't hang about in the rain.
Norma It's stopped now.
Ray Oh, Norma, I want you to meet Sheila Hilton.
Sheila (*nervously*) Hallo, Mrs Brent. Ray's told me so much about you.

Norma Has he?

Sheila Nice things, honestly. I've been admiring your house and your furniture. It's super. I'm fond of old-fash . . . I mean, antiques.

Norma Would you like a drink? (*Noticing the glasses*) Or have you already had one?

Ray Yes, but we wouldn't mind . . .

Norma Then you won't need another. All these glasses. (*She moves round, collecting glasses*) Have you been holding a party?

Ray Tony Marshall dropped in. I gave him a Scotch. Thought you'd approve.

Norma What did he want?

Ray A word with Stephen.

Norma Really?

Ray He needs some advice on the play he's producing. Oh, and he said he'd see you on Friday. At rehearsal.

Norma nods, then sees the hair-dryer

Norma What's my hair-dryer doing down here?

Sheila I borrowed it. I hope you don't mind. My hair got wet in the . . .

Ray (*putting his arm round Sheila*) I've got some good news for you, Norma. Sheila and I are going to get married.

Norma You're much too young. And Sheila can't be more than seventeen.

Sheila I'm eighteen!

Norma And what would you live on?

Ray Well—the money Great-grandfather left me.

Norma You can't manage on the interest as it is.

Ray I meant the capital.

Norma You can't touch that till you're twenty-five.

Ray But as trustee you could advance me a couple of thousand.

Norma Sorry. I suggest you have a nice, long engagement.

Sheila We can't.

Norma Can't?

Sheila We have to get married soon.

Norma Really? Did you run out of pills?

Sheila Please help me, Mrs Brent. We've seen a flat . . .

Ray We have to buy the fittings and fixtures to get it, and we need money for furniture. We need money now.

Norma (*pouring herself a drink; not interested*) Oh, yes?

Sheila If we lose this place, it'll be hard to find anything.

Norma Ray will have his money when he's older and more responsible.

Ray I'm responsible now.

Norma (*looking at Sheila*) H'm, are you?

Ray Yes, I bloody am!

Norma I'm rather tired, so if you don't mind . . .

Ray We do mind. It's *my* money, I've a right to it.

Norma If you spend it you'll lose the interest, then you'll be back here, trying to borrow from me all over again. (*She turns away*)

Ray If you say "No", I'll go to Stephen.

Norma He doesn't approve of his students sleeping around.

Ray Does he approve of his *wife* sleeping around?

Norma swings round, glaring

Norma *Wha-at* did you say?

Ray All right, Norma, I know, so let's cut the corners, eh? No more patronizing . . .

Norma What do you know?

Ray I know why you took away my key when I was living here.

Norma I needed it. I'd lost mine.

Ray So you said.

Norma And I wanted you out of the place.

Ray Naturally.

Norma You were becoming a pest and a bore.

Ray You threw me out because I was in the way, and you were scared I might walk in and catch you at it. (*To Sheila*) She wanted the place to herself. Even the poor old daily got the boot. And we all know why, don't we, Norma?

Norma How dare you speak to me like that!

Ray There's no truth in it, then?

Norma None!

Ray So you won't mind if I tell Stephen?

Norma Tell him what, for God's sake?

Ray Well, about your little trip to Cheltenham.

Norma (*startled*) Wha-at?

Ray I've got proof. You stayed at the Green Flag Hotel with lover boy.

Norma That's a filthy lie!

Ray Don't panic. (*Smiling insolently*) I won't tell Stephen—if you advance me that couple of thousand now.

Norma Don't you dare threaten me!

Norma slaps Ray viciously across the face. Sheila gasps and rushes to him

Now get to hell out of here! And take that cheap little tart with you!

Sobbing, Sheila runs off to the hall

Norma mounts the stairs. Ray goes below the gallery

Ray You'll be sorry you called her that, bloody sorry! You cow! (*Hurrying to the hall*) Sheila! Sheila! Wait for me!

Norma (*loudly*) And don't you come back here, trying to blackmail me!

Stephen appears in the hall with a suitcase and briefcase. He is mature, attractive, with a strong personality and charm. He looks at Ray in astonishment as the boy rushes past him

Ray Can't stop, Stephen. See you.

Ray rushes out

Stephen gazes after him, puzzled, then comes into the room and sees Norma. He drops his suitcase and briefcase

Stephen What *is* this—a Peace Conference?

Norma throws her wrap over the gallery and descends to greet him with a brief kiss

Norma Stephen, how marvellous. I didn't expect you till much later tonight.

Stephen I caught an earlier plane. Who was the girl?

Norma One of Ray's pick-ups.

Stephen She looked upset. What's been going on? I heard you shouting "blackmail".

Norma looks wary. To avoid his scrutiny, she moves behind him to help remove his raincoat

Norma Ray goaded me into losing my temper.

Stephen Blackmail's a strong word.

Norma (*forcing a laugh*) Darling, he was pestering me, as usual, for his capital. I said it was . . . just like blackmail.

Stephen Is that all?

Norma Of course. Why didn't you let me know you'd be back early? I could have met you at the airport.

Stephen (*moving to the desk*) I did ring. There was no reply.

Norma I was at the Hendersons. Dinner party. Rather dull. I'd have welcomed an excuse to get out of it.

Norma goes to the hall to hang his coat in the closet. He sits at the desk to open his letters

Stephen I called Joan. She said she'd give you the message when you came in.

Norma I wasn't told. (*Returning*) Anyway, you're back, that's the main thing. How are the parents?

Stephen (*reading his letters*) Fine.

Norma Did your lectures go well?

Stephen They didn't hurl any missiles. (*He sees the note in Plato and reads it*)

Norma I wrote that in case I was out or in bed when you got home. Now —can I get you a meal?

Stephen I dined on the flight. I could use a drink, though.

Norma Bourbon? (*Going to the cabinet*) How are you feeling—after your accident?

Stephen (*moving to the fireplace*) Who told you?

Norma Diane. She rang me from London this afternoon. Said you'd been in a pile-up in a hired car in New York. Were you badly hurt?

Stephen Slight concussion. Rather shaken, that's all.

Norma Enough, surely, You didn't mention it in your letters, darling.

Stephen I didn't think it was that important.

Norma (*giving him his drink*) And you also forgot to mention you'd run into Diane in New York. Quite a coincidence, wasn't it, both being there at the same time. (*She sits on the settee with her own drink*)

Stephen She flew over to see her American publishers.

Norma Really? And how did you meet?

Stephen At a literary party in Greenwich Village. (*Tasting his drink*) You've forgotten, I don't take it neat. Maybe you confused me with someone else.

Stephen adds soda to his glass. Norma looks away, her expression guarded

Norma Diane said she visited you in hospital.

Stephen Yes.

Norma (*acidly*) And when you were discharged—I suppose you took her out on the town?

Stephen Why not? She *is* a member of the family.

Norma *My* family, not yours. There's a subtle distinction.

Stephen It was good to have company. New York can be a lonely place.

Norma Well, I'm glad *you* weren't lonely. *I* was.

Stephen (*sceptically*) Were you?

There is a knock on the front door. Stephen glances out of the window

Norma (*rising*) Now who can that . . .

Stephen Cliff and Joan.

Norma Oh, hell, no!

Stephen Late to call, isn't it?

Norma God, who'd have neighbours? Get rid of them.

Stephen exits to the hall

Norma mounts the stairs, pausing half-way up to listen

Cliff (*off*) We saw your taxi and . . .

Stephen (*off*) Come along in.

Joan (*off*) Just for a few minutes, then.

Norma sighs and descends the stairs, putting on a social smile

Joan and Cliff Prior enter ahead of Stephen. Cliff is a conversion builder, rugged, in his early forties. Joan, his wife, is a homely person

Cliff Hope we're not barging in at an awkward time, Norma. Just wanted to say welcome back to Stephen.

Norma Do sit down.

Stephen (*going to the cabinet*) What'll you drink?

Joan Nothing for me, thanks. (*She sits on the settee*)

Stephen Cliff?

Cliff indicates a small drink and joins Stephen at the cabinet

Cliff Enjoy your trip or vacation or whatever you call it?

Stephen Yes, though it wasn't entirely a vacation. I worked, too.

Norma And he appeared on television. He must be quite a celebrity over there now.

Stephen Everyone goes on TV in the States. With so many channels, they have to scout around to find enough recruits.

Cliff Anyway, it must feel good to be home again.

Joan Unless you think of America as "home". Have you ever wanted to go back and live there—permanently, I mean?

Norma After seven years here? No, you wouldn't ever want to leave England, would you, darling?

Stephen Don't lay bets on it.

Cliff What made you settle in England?

Stephen I came over on a six months' exchange basis between the two universities.

Norma Then he was offered the Chair for American studies here.

Stephen It seemed a good opportunity—at the time.

Norma He also met *me*.

Cliff That really clinched it, eh?

Norma Actually, he knew my cousin Diane first. She introduced us. (*Acidly*) And by the strangest coincidence he ran into her in New York on this trip. (*To Stephen*) I wonder you didn't have her with you on the TV chat show, darling, or did you?

Stephen Diane won't go on television.

Norma No, might spoil the image of a crime novelist. She prefers to be shadowy, mysterious.

Joan I've often wondered why we never see her photograph on the back of book jackets. Her novels are very good, aren't they?

Norma M'm—if you like that kind of thing.

Joan Does she ever come here?

Norma No, she's too busy flying round the world, pursuing—(*looking at Stephen*)—material for her work.

Joan I envy anyone that sort of life. I wanted to have a holiday abroad this summer, but Cliff was too busy to get away.

Stephen Finding plenty of properties to convert?

Cliff (*sitting beside Joan*) Can't handle them all.

Norma I wish you'd get around to extending my kitchen. I'm driven mad trying to cook in that mousehole.

Stephen Are you doing the cooking now? Where's our Mrs Sullivan?

Norma I got rid of her. Too slapdash. You did promise, Cliff, when you sold us this place, that you'd . . .

Cliff I'll start the work as soon as I can. But we're way behind schedule now. And you should see the trouble I have with the men. They'll strike if there's not enough *sugar* in their tea.

The others smile politely

I'd like to throw it all in and escape to a desert island.

Norma That wouldn't suit *you*, would it, Joan?

Joan God, no! I'd go round the bend, being far away from town life and the shops. That reminds me, Berridges have a sale tomorrow. I want to get there early before the best bargains are snapped up. Coming?

Norma Not this time. I'm washing my hair in the morning.

Joan I did mine this afternoon.

Norma (*unflatteringly*) *Did* you, dear?

Stephen And it looks great, Joan. (*He sits at his desk, putting a hand to his forehead*)

Joan Are you feeling all right, Stephen?

Stephen Headache, that's all.

Norma (*moving to him*) Poor darling, he had a car crash in New York and he's been suffering from headaches and nightmares ever since. He's even started walking in his sleep.

Stephen Diane seems to have given you the lowdown.

Joan (*rising*) We mustn't keep you any longer. Come on, Cliff. (*Sharply*) Come on!

Cliff We've only just got here. (*He finishes his drink*)

Joan Stephen's tired. (*Looking at Norma*) You must both come to dinner one evening. It's ages since we had a rubber of bridge.

Stephen (*rising*) That would be very pleasant.

Joan moves to the hall archway with Norma. Cliff follows

Cliff I'll get started on that kitchen the first chance I . . .

Stephen Don't bother.

Cliff But Norma keeps saying . . .

Stephen I know, but we'll skip it.

Cliff shrugs, puzzled. Norma looks even more astonished, throwing a glance at Stephen before she sees Joan and Cliff out

Norma, Joan and Cliff exit

Joan (*off*) Pity you can't come to Berridges sale.

Norma (*off*) Show me your bargains when you get back. Good night.

Norma returns

Berridge's sale! The excitement would kill me!

Stephen picks up his suitcase and mounts the stairs

Norma What was that about the kitchen? You know I want it extended. I've been nagging Cliff for ages.

Stephen We may not be staying.

Norma First I've heard of it.

Stephen (*pausing on the gallery*) I was offered a lectureship in New York.

Norma You haven't accepted?

Stephen I have time to consider.

Norma And you expect me to live over there?

Stephen I expect you to do exactly as you please. Good night. I'll sleep in the guest room.

Norma Why?

Stephen I'm flaked out.

Norma Why don't you want to sleep with me?

Stephen I've had an exhausting journey, so if you don't mind . . .

Norma I do mind! You've been away for weeks and the first night back you want us to sleep apart. It's Diane, isn't it? What went on in New York?

Stephen She was kind to me.

Norma Kind! How bloody kind?

Stephen I'm not in the mood for one of your slanging matches. (*He turns away to continue upstairs*)

Norma (*striding to the side of the staircase*) Did you carry your intellectual discussions up into the hotel bedroom? Diane said you'd been sleep-walking. How did she know that?

Stephen I told her, of course.

Norma You didn't have to tell her. She knew. She knew because she was in the same damned bed with you!

Stephen No! We stayed at different hotels.

Norma God, how she must have drained you!

Stephen That's enough. We'll finish this in the morning.

Norma We'll finish it now! (*Swinging away*) That slut chasing you to New York like a . . .

Stephen Cut it out!

Norma It's true, isn't it?

Stephen puts down his case and descends the stairs. She backs away from him warily

Stephen You're the one who should be answering *my* questions. (*He takes a cable from his pocket*)

Norma What's that?

Stephen An anonymous cable. It reached me at The Manhattan Hotel. It's postmarked London. (*Reading*) "Your wife having an affair. Advise you take immediate action to avoid scandal."

Norma (*snatching the cable*) This is libel! I could sue!

Stephen Oh? Then you know who sent it?

Norma Of course I damn well don't!

Stephen Then how could you sue? Shall I take it to the police?

Norma No, don't do that.

Stephen Why not? If you've nothing to hide . . .

Norma Are you going to take the word of some filthy poison pen writer?

Stephen Why should anyone send me a libellous cable—if there's no truth in it?

Norma One of your students, perhaps. They'll do anything for a rag. (*Suddenly*) Ray, of course! That spiteful little sod!

Stephen You're getting an obsession about the boy. Why should he do this?

Norma To hurt me, of course.

Stephen Figure it out. He'd have to go to a lot of trouble and expense, make a special journey to London to send it. Take a look at the postmark. Want me to tackle him?

Norma (*screwing up the cable*) Forget the whole damned thing!

Stephen I can't do that—because it isn't all. Diane said that you . . .

Norma My God, she really went to town on me!

Stephen When you stayed with her in Cornwall last August, you told me it was for the whole week.

Norma (*turning away*) It was.

Stephen But you left her cottage on the Friday morning, and you didn't get back till Monday. Where did you spend that weekend? (*Pause*) *Where*, Norma?

Norma I've told you. I was with *her*!

Stephen Next time you lie, think up a good one.

Norma You bastard! You prefer to believe that bitch! Well, I know her better than you do. She's always been jealous of me, wildly jealous because I took you away from her. And she's never got over Grandfather's money coming to *me*!

Stephen Diane didn't give a damn for that legacy. She earns more than enough from her novels. But I wish the inheritance *had* gone to her. It changed you.

Norma Yes, thank God. I'm independent now. I can do as I please.

Stephen And that includes—taking a lover.

Norma You wouldn't care if I did, apart from the scandal. And scandal is something you can't take. Nothing must damage your precious image up at the university. It's all you care about. You're cold and indifferent and a bloody big bore, and I'm sick to death of you! I need a man, a man, who needs *me*!

Stephen So you admit it. You've found yourself one.

Norma And if I have—what could you do about it?

She picks up a decanter. He wrests it from her and replaces it

Stephen Finish with him! While you're my wife you'll stop whoring around and behave decently!

Norma And what's behaving decently? You going to bed with Diane?

She brushes past him. He catches her hand and swings her round

Stephen I'm warning you, Norma . . .

Norma To hell with your threats! (*She jerks herself free and storms round to the back of the settee, turning to point to him*)

Norma Just try to make trouble and I'll divorce you, citing Diane.

Stephen I won't have her involved.

Norma I'll make bloody sure she is! I'll drag you and that bitch through the divorce court, and by the time I've finished with you both your names will stink to high heaven!

Stephen You're sick. (*He turns off the electric fire*)

Norma Are you in love with her. Are you?

He turns towards the stairs. She rages after him

Answer me, damn you! Are you in love with her—or was she just an easy lay?

Stephen Good night.

Norma (*hysterically*) My God, you have the damned nerve to criticize me, when you and my bloody cousin have been shacking up in some hotel bedroom!

Stephen (*shaking her*) Stop it, stop it at once!

Norma (*struggling*) Go to hell! I'm going to cut you and that bitch out of my will!

Stephen I don't give a rap for your money. Now finish with this man, or I'll find out who he is . . . then I'll deal with him.

Stephen flings her into a chair and goes rapidly upstairs, picking up his case

Norma rises, goes to the phone, glances upstairs, then puts on a record to cover the sound of her phone call. Dramatic music is heard, softly played. Norma dials, then speaks into the receiver

Norma It's me, darling. I've just had a flaming row with Stephen . . . Oh, some busybody sent him a cable, saying I was having an affair, and now he means to find out who you are . . . We must get away . . . Tomorrow. I'll divorce him, citing my cousin Diane, then you and I can get . . . Well, do as I suggested . . . Yes. Meet me at the Green Flag Hotel about six. I shall see my solicitor in the morning . . . To change my will. I want to leave everything to *you*, darling. Everything. 'Till tomorrow. 'Bye.

Norma replaces receiver, looking triumphant, turns off record player, then takes a key from the bag, unlocks desk drawer, and takes out a small deed box. Then she switches off lights at the garden door and goes upstairs with the deed box

After a pause, the landing light goes out

Pause. The garden door opens slowly, curtains billow in the breeze. Ray enters the darkened room, the hood of his windcheater up. He flashes a torch up the stairs, pausing to listen. Silence. Slowly he moves into the room and shines his torch on the hair-dryer as—

the CURTAIN *falls*

SCENE 2

The same. Wednesday, 9.15 a.m.

The window curtains are drawn back and sunshine illumines the room. There

is a knock on the front door. Stephen enters from the dining-room archway
with a coffee cup. He puts this on his desk and exits to the hall

Sheila (*off*) Sorry to bother you so early, but . . .
Stephen That's okay. Come along in.

Sheila and Stephen enter from the hall

Sheila I don't suppose you remember me . . .
Stephen Oh, yes, I do. You brushed past me last night in one hell of a hurry.
Ray's girl friend?
Sheila Right.
Stephen Well, now, what can I do for you?
Sheila I've come to fetch my jacket. I left it drying on that chair. (*She sees
it has gone*) Oh . . .
Stephen Not there now. Maybe my wife hung it in the hall closet. Care to
take a look?

Sheila exits to the hall

Stephen opens a desk drawer—not the locked one—and puts some papers
into his briefcase

Any luck?
Sheila (*off*) No, I can't see it.
Stephen Hang on. (*He goes to the stairs*) Norma!
Norma (*off, upstairs*) What is it? I'm doing my hair.
Stephen Ray's young friend is here. She left her jacket behind last night.
Any idea where it is?
Norma (*off*) No!

Sheila enters from the hall

Sheila Don't worry, Ray must have taken it with him.
Stephen Didn't he catch you up?
Sheila No. He had his car and I took that short cut across the park. I was
upset, I just wanted to be on my own for a bit.
Stephen You'd had a fight?
Sheila Not with *him*. (*She glances towards the stairs*)
Stephen Oh, I see.

Norma comes down in a white housecoat and white towel/turban: no rings
or watch

Norma Oh, Sheila. Found your jacket?
Stephen No, she hasn't.
Sheila Perhaps Ray did pick it up before he left.
Stephen You're quite sure you didn't take it upstairs, Norma?

Norma Why should I do that? Perhaps *you* moved it, while walking in your sleep. I thought I heard someone moving about down here. (*She pours herself a vodka and tomato juice*)

Stephen Wouldn't breakfast do you more good?

Norma This *is* breakfast—a Bloody Mary.

Sheila Well, I'd better go or I'll be late for the office.

Stephen Where is the office?

Sheila Bradshaw and Webb, the estate agents in the High Street.

Stephen I pass there on my way to the university. I'll give you a lift.

Sheila That's very kind of you. Thanks.

Stephen (*patting her shoulder in passing*) Stick around, I'll get the car out.

Stephen exits to the hall

Norma lounges full-length on the settee to read the morning newspaper

Sheila About last night, Mrs Brent . . .

Norma Yes?

Sheila I'm sorry. I mean, for rushing off the way I did. I hope you didn't think I was being rude.

Norma Don't you remember? I asked you to go.

Sheila I was very upset.

Norma Obviously.

Sheila Don't hold it against Ray. I mean, for all those things he said. He didn't mean them, he was just talking wildly. Well, you know Ray.

Norma Yes, I know Ray—to my cost.

Sheila We're so worried. (*She sits on the arm of the armchair*) We have to get married soon and—well, how can we without any money?

Norma You should have thought of that before playing—mothers and fathers.

Sheila I've a little in my post office book but nothing like enough. If Ray apologizes will it make any difference?

Norma No, it won't.

Sheila (*flopping into the chair*) But my parents, I don't know what they'll say when they find out. Dad's so narrow-minded, and with a shop in the town he couldn't bear it if—if people started gossiping about me.

Norma That's *your* problem, not mine.

Sheila (*crying*) I don't know what we can do.

Norma Ray is far too young to get married.

Sheila But the baby . . .

Norma Get rid of it!

Sheila (*rising*) No!

Norma If you want a lift to work you'd better go now.

Sheila We love each other, really we do.

Norma Then you won't mind waiting.

Sheila We can't wait, we can't!

Norma continues reading the paper

Please, Mrs Brent, please, please help us.

Norma shakes her head and waves Sheila away

Oh, God!

Sobbing, Sheila runs out through the hall

Norma pulls the telephone to the settee and dials

Norma (*into the phone*) Mr Corby senior, please . . . Mrs Stephen Brent . . . Hallo, Mr Corby, may I call at your office this morning? It's about my will. I want to change it . . . No, not a codicil. I want new documents drawn up, cutting out all previous beneficiaries. I'm leaving everything to one person . . . Half past eleven? I'll be there. 'Bye. (*She replaces the receiver and picks up the newspaper*)

Stephen enters from the hall

Forgot something?

Stephen My briefcase. (*He picks it up*) The poor kid's crying out there. She won't tell me what's wrong.

Norma She's pregnant.

Stephen Oh heck, no!

Norma Yes.

Stephen And Ray's responsible?

Norma So she says. Now she expects him to marry her. Ridiculous, isn't it?

Stephen Well, of course he *must* marry her, poor girl.

Norma Save your sympathy. It's obvious she worked the whole thing. Believed Ray would be a good catch, so she's using the oldest trick in the world.

Stephen They need help now, not criticism.

Norma Trust you to stand up for the young.

Stephen We must fix the wedding.

Norma Ray can't afford to get married.

Stephen Release part of his legacy, then.

Norma He can wait till he's twenty-five. If he's so keen to marry the girl he can leave the university and get a job.

Stephen Don't you give a damn for anyone but yourself?

Norma (*dreamily*) Oh, yes. Yes, I do.

Stephen I see. So you mean to continue with this sordid affair?

Norma That's *my* business.

Stephen Mine, too, I should have thought. I've decided to accept the New York lectureship. Maybe then we can make a fresh start.

Norma turns her head away indifferently. He takes a gift-wrapped package from his briefcase

I forgot to give you this last night.

He hands it to her. She glances at it, then tosses it across the settee

Norma Give it to Diane.

Stephen (*after a pause; slowly*) That's the last present I'll ever buy you.

He turns to go. Norma rises and points to her star predictions in the paper

Norma My stars say I'm going on a journey. Suppose I told you I *am* going on a journey—what would you say?

Stephen (*turning in the archway to the hall*) Good-bye, Norma.

Stephen exits through the hall

Norma glares after him. She puts on the record, turning it up loud, and sways to the music as she wanders back to the side of the settee. She picks up the dryer and switches it on, then screams and tumbles back over the arm of the settee, then rolls on to the floor, still grasping the lethal dryer. She lies still, as—

the CURTAIN *falls*

SCENE 3

The same. A week later, early evening

The room is lit by fading daylight, which dims until Stephen switches on the lights. As the CURTAIN *rises he is discovered, dressed in a sober black suit and tie, speaking on the phone*

Stephen Tell the Vice-Chancellor I'm sorry I couldn't keep my appointment this afternoon. The inquest dragged on and I've only just got back. Find out if he can see me tomorrow, about ten . . . I haven't any tutorials until eleven-thirty . . .

Joan enters from the dining-room archway with a tray of tea-things. She wears a hat and suit

Stephen Thank you, Miss Thatcher, see you in the morning. (*He replaces the receiver*)

Joan You're not going back to work already?

Stephen Tomorrow.

Joan (*putting the tray on a low table*) It's far too soon.

Stephen I've had a week off, that's more than enough.

Joan (*sitting on the settee*) Well, I don't think so. Not with all the distress and anxiety you've had.

Stephen Work takes my mind off. Thanks for bothering. (*He indicates the tea tray*)

Joan It's nothing. (*Pouring tea*) I was at the doctor's yesterday and I told him Cliff and I were very worried about you.

Stephen Why?

Joan The shock and everything. Dr Webster agreed that you ought to take a really long holiday, get right away from this house and the town.

Stephen I'm not in the mood for a holiday.

Joan You know what I mean—a rest, change of atmosphere.

Stephen Work suits me better, absorbs my mind. (*He moves to the desk with his tea*)

Joan May I phone Cliff?

Stephen Of course.

Joan (*dialling*) I expect he's still down at the site office. The hours he puts in. He says it's the only way to run a business these days.

Stephen Better tell him the verdict.

Joan I have. I rang him after the hearing. (*Pause*) What'll happen now?

Stephen That's up to the police.

Stephen sees the note sticking out of the book. He takes it out and reads it. Joan replaces the receiver

Joan No answer, he must be on his way home. What's the matter? You look as though you've seen . . .

Stephen I've just found this. (*He hands her the note*)

Joan (*reading*) "I shall come back." It's signed "Norma".

Stephen (*quietly*) Yes. Signed—Norma.

Joan But . . . Oh, she must have written this ages ago. You just hadn't noticed it before.

Stephen Look at the date. (*He pours himself a Scotch*)

Joan Today's. But it can't mean . . .

Stephen It means someone has broken in here, and is having a morbid little joke at my expense.

Joan Surely nobody we know would—well—how could they get in? You don't go out and leave doors and windows open, do you?

Stephen No. Yet I sometimes return and—(*he looks around slowly*)—feel uneasy. As though I'm not . . . alone here.

Joan You're imagining it. Of course if Cliff had died suddenly, tragically, the way Norma has, I'd feel disturbed.

Stephen You believe in the supernatural?

Joan Not really. Coming back after death and all that. You don't think there's anything in it, do you?

Stephen There are so many things beyond our comprehension in the universe.

Joan Tear up that note, forget all about it. I'm sure it's just a mindless hoax.

Stephen sits at the typewriter and types a few words, then compares them with the note

Was it written on your machine?

Stephen (*nods*) The same copperplate type.

Joan Then someone could have broken in when we were at the inquest.

Stephen Unless—Norma did type it herself.

Joan Stephen!

Stephen Isn't there such a thing as—automatic writing? A spirit working through someone else?

Joan I've heard of such things. Not that I've ever taken them very seriously

Stephen Could *I* have been used as a medium?

Joan You?

Stephen I've been sleep-walking. I did last night. Woke up and found myself at the garden door.

Joan Oh dear . . .

Stephen But before I woke up—could I have typed in my sleep?

Joan Without knowing it?

Stephen It's feasible.

Joan You must see Dr Webster. You need a tonic and a complete rest.

Stephen How could I go away, even if I wanted to? After that verdict there are bound to be more questions from the police. If I as much as packed a toothbrush they'd be suspicious, think I was about to skip the country.

Joan They can't imagine you've done anything.

Stephen The coroner wasn't satisfied, was he? And the police aren't, either. They took away the dryer, and it hasn't been returned.

There is a knock at the front door. Stephen pockets the note

Don't mention this to anyone.

Joan No, no, of course not.

Stephen exits to the hall. Joan takes the hot-water jug out through the kitchen and dining-room arch
    Stephen enters from the hall with Tony

Tony Just thought I'd drop around and—well, ask how things went today.

Stephen The jury returned an Open Verdict.

Tony That was unexpected, surely?

Stephen Yes.

Tony We discussed it at the golf club—you know how one does—and everyone felt it was bound to be "Death by Misadventure". An Open Verdict. Surprising. You have my sympathy, you know that.

Stephen Thanks.

Tony We miss her very much at the club. Everyone liked her. Always so warm and friendly—and she played a good game.

Stephen Yes.

Tony What are your plans now? Staying on here?

Stephen Haven't made up my mind.

Tony See how the wind blows, eh?

Stephen What's that imply?

Tony Nothing. Really no reason why you should leave the university—or resign from the golf club, either, no reason at all.

Stephen The committee want me to resign?

Tony No, no, why should they? Well, they don't know the verdict yet, anyway.

Stephen And when they do—they'll ask for my resignation?

Tony Believe me, Stephen, it wouldn't be *my* doing.

Stephen Let me jump the gun and resign now.

Tony Don't be a fool. In any case, there's no rush.

Stephen My reputation seems to be in the balance. Can't have anyone doubtful in the Royal Terrace golf club, can we?

Tony See how things turn out, eh?

Stephen I'll be writing to the committee.

Tony Oh?

Stephen To thank them for the wreath.

Joan enters with the water jug and more cups and saucers

Joan Mr Marshall, would you like a cup of tea?

Tony (*smiling*) With someone so charming to pour it out—yes, please.

There is a knock on the front door

Stephen Oh God, who's that?

Tony (*looking from the window*) There's a beat-up red sports car at the kerb.

Stephen Ray. I thought he'd gone to Sheila's place.

Stephen exits to the hall

Joan I hope that boy's got over his temper. The way he went for the coroner.

Tony Stephen's taken it hard, hasn't he?

Joan Yes. Well, he's been through so much. And all on top of that accident in New York.

Tony Accident? I didn't know. What happened?

Joan A car crash.

Tony Was he badly hurt?

Joan Concussion and shock. Now he's started sleep-walking.

Ray and Sheila enter from the hall. Stephen follows and switches on the lights

Ray God, I'd rather sit a dozen exams than go through that mud bath again.

Sheila Oh, belt up, Ray. He hasn't stopped since we left the inquest.

Ray What bloody right have they to pry into other people's affairs?

Tony Surely that's the whole point of a public inquiry?

Ray To dig the dirt, you mean, 'cos that's what that damned coroner was doing. He had the nerve to ask Stephen whether he was on good terms with his wife. Then he started badgering Sheila and me, bloody old . . .

Stephen Simmer down, Ray. (*To Joan*) I've left the door open for Cliff. He's putting his van in the garage. I told him you were here.

Joan Good. Would you young people like some tea?

Sheila No, thanks. We had some at my parents' place. We didn't stop long 'cos Ray and Dad got into an argument and I didn't want any more trouble.

Ray I'd like something stronger than tea.

Stephen Help yourself.

There is a distant roll of thunder. Ray helps himself to a Scotch, neat

Cliff enters from the hall, flicking rain from his jacket

Cliff Sounds like a storm getting up. Evening, everyone. (*He kisses Joan on the cheek*) Making yourself useful, dear? Marshall, glad you're here. I've been waiting for ages to get into your club. When does my name come to the top of the list? (*He sits beside Joan*)

Tony glances ceilingwards

Tony I'll take it up with the committee.

Ray That's right, chat about trivial matters, avoid the main issue.

Ray is about to pour himself another drink when Stephen takes the decanter away and replaces it, motioning Ray to sit down. He perches rebelliously on the arm of Sheila's chair

Sheila I told my dad about the inquest and he said British hair-dryers are the safest on the market—if people don't mess about with them.

Tony What exactly had gone wrong?

Stephen The forensic expert said, in evidence, that the dryer had been— tampered with.

Cliff In what way?

Stephen He wouldn't go into details.

Joan He explained that he was preparing a full report.

Stephen All he would say was that the damage done to the dryer—had turned it into a lethal object.

Tony Could Norma have found it didn't work and tried to mend it herself?

Stephen I doubt that.

Joan The coroner wanted to know if it had been in to a shop for repair recently.

Stephen It hadn't, I'd already checked the local electrical shops.

Sheila Yes, my dad *said* you'd been in.

Tony Sheila, *you* had the dryer when I called round . . .

Stephen You called that night?

Tony I thought you might be back from the States. I wanted a word with you about *Lysistrata*.

Stephen I see.

Tony Sheila used the dryer while I was here and it seemed to be working all right then.

Ray What are you suggesting—that she damaged it?

Tony She may have—accidentally.

Joan Perhaps she put it too close to her wet hair.

Cliff Or dropped it.

Sheila (*alarmed*) I didn't! Tell them I didn't, Ray.

Ray Of course she damn well didn't. What are you trying to do—pin this on *her*?

Stephen Cool it, Ray.

Ray (*rising*) I'm sick of you lot hammering away at Sheila. And all those loaded questions at the inquest. How the hell did that coroner know I'd get my inheritance when Norma died?

Stephen Everybody knows. You've made no secret of the fact.

Tony All obstacles are gone now, aren't they?

Ray What's that supposed to mean?

Tony You get your money. It's an ill wind . . .

Ray So that's what you're all thinking; that I stood to gain by her death.

Cliff Didn't you?

Joan Norma told me you used to run up bills on the strength of your legacy.

Tony As good as a Barclaycard.

Stephen Are you in debt, Ray?

Ray Who isn't?

Stephen Much?

Ray The instalments on my car are due, I have a writ from the gear shop and I'm fast running out of pot! Satisfied?

Cliff The police will ferret that lot out.

Tony Better have your answers ready.

Sheila Leave him alone! Why are you all digging at Ray? Anyone would think he . . .

Stephen Yes, Sheila?

Sheila Nothing. Nothing.

Stephen Well, now, there's been a new development, and one of you may be able to help me. Norma's bank manager told me she drew out two thousand pounds in five-pound notes recently.

Joan What for?

Stephen I don't know—yet.

Joan When we went shopping she always paid by cheque.

Stephen The money has disappeared and there's no evidence that Norma bought anything with it. Cliff, did she give you an advance?

Cliff Advance?

Stephen To buy materials for the kitchen extension.

Cliff No. In any case we were still at the drawing-board stage, and besides my estimates wouldn't have come to anything like two thousand pounds. And I wouldn't have sent in the account until the work was finished.

Stephen How about you, Ray? Did Norma give you any cash recently?

Ray You've got to be joking! She wouldn't let me touch my own capital, let alone dish out hers.

Stephen Are you sure?

Ray God, yes, I'm sure. If I'd had that sort of loot would I still be in debt? Well, would I?

Sheila She wouldn't do a thing to help us. And she knew we hadn't a hope of getting married without some money.

Tony And now it's all very convenient. No problems.

Ray You snide bastard!

Joan He's only stating a fact, Ray.

Sheila (*emotionally*) You think we wanted it this way, wanted Mrs Brent dead so that Ray would get his legacy? If that's on your minds why don't you say so? (*Going to Stephen*) You think I caused your wife's death, don't you? Don't you?

Stephen There's no point in upsetting yourself, Sheila.

Sheila (*sobbing*) Well, I didn't, I didn't! Tell them I didn't, Ray. (*She clings to Ray*) Tell them.

Joan Nobody's accused you, Sheila.

Ray Haven't they? You think we're both in it, don't you? (*Silence. To Sheila*) Come on, love, we're getting out of here.

Ray leads Sheila to the hall archway, then turns to face the others

Ray And in future do me a favour, will you? All mind your own bloody business and leave us alone!

Ray and Sheila exit to the hall

Tony Sorry about that. Seems I triggered it off.

Joan Poor Sheila. She's had a trying day. She was very distressed in the witness-box. I was afraid she was going to break down completely. I did feel sorry for her.

Cliff (*to Stephen*) Do you think Ray had that two thousand?

Stephen No, or he'd have been flashing it around, spending freely. I suppose you haven't a clue about it, Tony?

Tony Me? Why, no.

Stephen It's costly to mount a classical production. I wondered if your committee had asked Norma to help finance the project?

Tony If they had I'd have known about it.

Stephen Just a thought.

The phone rings. Stephen answers it

   Tudor Gables . . . Yes, speaking.

Joan Give me a hand, Cliff.

Joan and Cliff carry the tea-things out to the hall

There is a knock on the front door

Tony I'll get it.

Tony goes out to the hall

Stephen (*into the phone*) Oh, hallo, Inspector . . . Yes, sure, when? . . . No, I'd rather come to you. What time? . . . Okay, I'll be there. Good-bye. (*He replaces the receiver, looking thoughtful*)

Joan and Cliff return. Tony appears in the hall archway

Stephen That was Detective-Inspector Neville. He wants to see me around half past eight this evening.
Cliff What for?
Stephen He didn't say.
Joan Why not come next door for a meal with us first? Would you care to join us, Mr Marshall?
Tony Thanks, but I'm dining with Colonel Fenwick.
Stephen Who was at the door?
Tony A reporter from the *Chronicle*.
Stephen (*turning off the fire*) That's all I need.
Tony It's all right, I got rid of him. But he may hang around outside.
Cliff Then we'd better go out by the garden. You can come through our house, too, Marshall, if you like.

They all move towards the garden door. There are three knocks on the front door

Joan Don't answer it. Come on.

Joan leads the way out into the garden, Cliff and Tony following

Three more knocks are heard. Stephen pauses, his hand on the light switch. Then he turns out the lights by the garden door

Stephen exits, closing the garden door after him. There is a pause, then a figure in white, hair concealed by a white head scarf, appears from the hall and moves into the cross beam of moonlight

The light illuminates the figure's face, leaving the rest in shadow, and giving an ethereal, ghostly appearance. There is a flash of lightning, and a rumble of thunder. The figure in white hovers, quite still now. The resemblance is so striking that it could be—the spirit of Norma

CURTAIN

ACT II

Scene 1

The same. Four hours later

In the room, lit only by the desk lamp, Diane Winslow is seated, typing a note. She is Norma's cousin, a crime novelist; attractive, intelligent, strongly resembling Norma in appearance, apart from her hair colouring. Her dark hair is hidden by the white head scarf seen on her in the previous Act, and her white raincoat shows she was the same person glimpsed before

Stephen enters from the hall and stops abruptly

Stephen Norma!

Diane (*swinging round in her chair*) Hallo, Stephen. (*She pulls off the head scarf and goes to him, hands outstretched*)

Stephen (*with relief*) Oh, Diane! With that scarf on—well, you looked just like . . .

He puts on the main lights, then takes her in his arms and they kiss lingeringly. It is an emotional moment for them both. After a while he helps to remove her raincoat

Oh, darling, you made it. I kinda hoped you might. God, how I've missed you.

Diane I've missed you, too, love—like hell.

Stephen You know, I wrote a week ago, when all this happened, but you didn't reply. I've rung your cottage several times since.

Diane I wasn't there. As soon as I got back from New York I had to fly to Stockholm.

Stephen Why Stockholm?

Diane The Swedes are turning one of my novels into a television serial. (*Standing back to look at him*) You look so worn, darling, as if you hadn't slept.

Stephen I haven't. I seem to have been swept around in a carousel. My whole life has been loused up by this tragic business.

Diane I know, I felt so guilty when I got back to Cornwall—and found your letter.

Stephen You—guilty?

Diane Well, because I hadn't been here to help. I can't believe I'll never see Norma again. She was so full of life . . .

Stephen We won't talk about it now.

He leads her to the settee and they sit close together, his arm around her

Stephen Did you come by car?

Diane No, train. Quicker from Cornwall. I got here a few hours ago and knocked several times. No response, so I let myself in.

Stephen How?

Diane I had a key. Norma left it behind on her last visit to me.

Stephen You haven't been waiting here all that time?

Diane No, no. I went to the Mitre for dinner. Oh, and I've booked a room there.

Stephen Why not stay here? Plenty of space.

Diane And plenty of scope for village gossip, too. I don't care but you do have to live and work in this town. And so soon after the accident . . .

Stephen makes a dismissing gesture

What's the matter?

Stephen It *wasn't* an accident.

Diane Not? But in your letter you said . . .

Stephen I thought so at first, then the inquest threw out that idea. They returned an open verdict.

Diane Did they indeed?

Stephen And now the police are treating it as—murder.

Diane Murder? Oh, my God.

Stephen rises, goes to the cabinet and pours drinks

Stephen Inspector Neville's handling the investigation. He wanted to see me this evening. I've just come from his office.

Diane He doesn't suspect *you*?

Stephen I don't know. He was very polite, too polite. Isn't the husband always the first line of inquiry?

Diane As a rule—unless he has an alibi.

Stephen Well, I haven't.

Diane What questions did he ask?

Stephen Subtle ones, sounding me out. Plenty of trip wires.

Diane You stepped over them, I hope.

Stephen Tried to. He wanted to know if Norma and I got along in the matrimonial stakes. I didn't say we'd had a violent row the evening before she died.

Diane A row—what about?

Stephen (*giving her a drink*) You, mainly. You'd phoned her and said we'd been seeing each other in New York.

Diane Sorry. Tactless of me. Only I thought you'd tell her when you got back.

Stephen The scene she made, going on and on and calling you names.

Diane Charming. Did you show her the cable?

Stephen Yes, and she admitted in the end that she had a lover, though she wouldn't name him. When I was upstairs I thought I heard the phone being replaced down here, so she could have been calling him to mention the quarrel.

Diane That's dicey. I suppose he hasn't surfaced—you know, stranger at the funeral?

Stephen There were quite a few people I didn't know. But then not all Norma's friends were mine.

Diane Perhaps he had good reason to stay in the background. Lovers do kill their mistresses.

Stephen And husbands kill their wives.

Diane (*rising*) We won't go into that.

Stephen The boy friend may stay away from the police, yet he could swing things—to throw suspicion on someone else.

Diane You?

Stephen So I could be up on a murder charge.

Diane Oh, my God!

Stephen How would you handle a situation like this in one of your books?

Diane The first thing would be to marshal the facts. That's my Inspector Quayle's line. He believes . . .

Stephen You talk about him as if he's for real.

Diane He is to me. He believes it's the small incidents that build up to vitally important clues. Clues that could lead to the killer. Let me have the gen. First the death itself. You said in your letter she'd been electrocuted. How?

Stephen With her hair-dryer.

Diane looks startled

It had been tampered with. Tonight Inspector Neville read me the latest report passed on by the forensic expert.

Diane Can you remember what it said?

Stephen The report? (*He closes his eyes, doing a mental recall*) Yes, vaguely. The negative lead had been connected to the first metal screw in the dryer . . .

Diane And the positive linked to the second screw—via the switches in the handle?

Stephen (*astonished*) How did you know that?

Diane *I* once killed somebody with a hair-dryer.

Stephen That's it! All the way home it's been haunting me, the feeling that I'd heard—or read—the whole thing before—in detail.

Diane I expect you had. I gave Norma a copy of the book years ago.

Stephen What was the title?

Diane *Hazard.*

Stephen (*going to the bookshelf*) It must still be here, Norma never threw anything away.

Diane (*joining him*) The trouble I went to, plagueing electricians to work out the details for me.

Stephen *Hazard* by Diane Winslow. (*He takes a book from the shelf*)

Diane Final chapter, towards the end. Inspector Quayle explaining how the murder was premeditated.

Stephen (*flipping over the pages*) Ah, here it is—"positive linked to the second screw via the switches in the handle . . .". Strange, the exact words you used a few moments ago.

Diane I do have total recall, darling.

Stephen (*reading on*) "And when the current was switched on, the effect would be lethal."

Diane (*moving away to the mantelpiece*) My God, she was killed by a method straight out of one of my books.

Stephen So what? Crime novels are full of ways to kill people.

Diane But this was so detailed. I've given someone a perfect blueprint for murder!

Stephen You couldn't have known anyone would copy it.

Diane If that book gets into the hands of the police . . .

Stephen They could set their sights on *you*!

Diane Or *you*! (*Pause*) Of course, I did write the book many years ago, only this copy is in *your* house, where it happened.

Stephen You must go away. I can't have you involved.

Diane I'm not leaving you, darling. We're going to solve this together. Now—who'd want to kill her?

Stephen I don't know.

Diane When did it happen?

Stephen The morning after I got back from New York.

Diane And the murderer could have tinkered with the dryer at almost any time, I suppose?

Stephen M'm. (*Pause*) No, wait. It was used the night before by young Sheila, Ray's girl friend. And left on that table. (*He points*)

Diane So it must have been fixed some time during that night.

Stephen By someone who got in while we were asleep.

Diane Who has a key?

Stephen I have. So have *you*, darling.

Diane Yes. Inspector Quayle would put me on his list, too. Who else? The daily help?

Stephen Norma fired her while I was away. Yet *someone* else must have a key. Look, I found this—today. (*He takes the note from his pocket*) It was typed on that machine and tucked into my copy of Plato.

Diane goes to him and reads the note

Diane "I shall come back. Norma."

Stephen And today's date.

Diane Hold on. (*She goes to the desk and takes another note from the same book*)

Stephen Another one?

Diane I don't know, I didn't read it. I noticed it when I was typing. I thought it was a book marker. (*She hands it to him*)

Stephen They're becoming a habit (*Reading it*) This one accuses me of murder.

Diane Don't let it shake you, darling. I know all these tricks. Someone's trying to throw suspicion away from themselves. Find out who's writing these notes—and you may discover the killer. Suspects, please. This girl who used the dryer? (*She sits at the desk, picks up a notebook and pencil and scribbles down the names*)

Stephen Sheila Hilton. She and Ray had called to see Norma, to tell her they had to get married.

Diane Had to? Oh, trust Ray.

Stephen She did.

Diane (*smiling faintly*) Who else?

Stephen While the young people were here Tony Marshall dropped in.

Diane Who's he?

Stephen Secretary of the golf club. Eligible bachelor.

Diane Why was he here that night?

Stephen He drops in on one pretext or another. Wanted a word with me about a Greek play he's producing.

Diane And no-one else, apart from you and Norma and, of course, Ray, could have known the dryer was down here?

Stephen Hang on. The Priors called—our next door neighbours. They didn't stay long.

Diane Long enough to see the dryer?

Stephen Sure. (*Indicating the table*) It was right there, a sitting target for anyone with murder in mind.

Diane Still, they'd have to know how to change over the leads and make it lethal. Did Norma get on with—what did you say their names are?

Stephen Cliff and Joan Prior. She called them dull but she went about with the wife, shopping, coffee mornings. Norma was rather patronizing towards Joan, considered her a back number.

Diane And the husband?

Stephen Cliff's a conversion builder. He turned a Tudor farmhouse into a pair of cottages, sold us this one and kept the other himself. Norma used to nag him about extending her kitchen, and I think he found it rather irritating.

Diane M'm. Nagging women often get their lot. So that gives your neighbours a motive. How about Ray?

Stephen He was quarrelling with Norma when I got home. She accused him of blackmail.

Diane Blackmailers like to keep their victims alive.

Stephen Sure. But don't forget he did stand to gain by her death. He's now free to control his own legacy, spend the capital, marry Sheila. No more begging and borrowing.

Diane And his girl friend—what do you know about her?

Stephen Only that she's a typist, lives with her parents, and her father has an electrical shop in the town.

Diane Then she may know something about electricity.

Stephen I hadn't considered that. But look, you can't suspect that kid . . .

Diane Inspector Quayle suspects everyone, even himself.

The telephone rings

Don't say I'm here.

Stephen (*on the phone*) Tudor Gab . . . Oh, hullo, Tony . . . Yes, I had a chat with him. Just routine inquiries, the usual drill . . . Sunday? M'm, I could do with some exercise. Ten-thirty okay? . . . Fine, see you on the links. (*He replaces the receiver*) Tony Marshall wanting to know how I got on with the police.

Diane Friendly interest—or morbid curiosity?

Stephen A little of both, I guess.

Diane What do you know about this Tony Marshall? Did he like Norma?

Stephen Oh sure, he admired her, thought her a good amateur actress, an asset to the golf club.

Diane Could he have been her lover?

Stephen Tony and Norma? It hadn't occurred to me.

Diane Let it simmer in your mind. He was so keen to find out how you'd got on with the police, he couldn't wait till morning. Had to ring you just now.

Stephen You make everything sound significant.

Diane Everything is: so Ray and his girl friend, your neighbours—the Priors—and Tony Marshall all saw the dryer down here that night. And any one of them could have come back and . . . (*She spreads her hands*)

Stephen So might I.

Diane Ye-es, so might you.

Stephen I had a motive and opportunity, let's face it. Inspector Neville asked me about my sleep-walking.

Diane How did he know?

Stephen People talk and the police latch on to any clue.

Diane Sell up, darling. Let's both go back to the States. Together.

Stephen I can't do that—yet. It would look as if I were running away. But there's nothing to keep *you* here.

Diane (*going to him; softly*) Isn't there?

Stephen (*holding her close*) You're tempting me. You know I love you like crazy, but . . .

Diane We're free now.

Stephen When this is all over.

Diane When. (*She shivers, looking round*) I feel we're not alone here.

Stephen You sense that, too? Every corner of the house, everything I touch reminds me of her. That exotic perfume she used still lingers in the air. In fact . . . (*He breaks off*)

Diane What?

Stephen On her dressing-table—the bottle was tipped over, the scent spilt . . .

Diane Stephen . . .

Stephen Yes, I know. I could have done it myself—while sleep-walking. Look, you can't stick around, you've got to get away from here.

Diane I don't want to leave you.

Stephen But the police will wonder what the set-up is between us.

Diane I'm one of the family.

Stephen They might put a different construction on it.

Diane I'll risk that.

Stephen (*moving away*) There's something I haven't told you. She was going to change her will.

Diane Leaving all her cash to her lover boy?

Stephen I guess so. She rang her solicitor that morning.

Diane How do you know that?

Stephen Corby told me after the inquest. She made an appointment to see him, but she died before she could reach his office.

Diane And she never named the boy friend?

Stephen No. Just told Corby over the phone that she wanted to leave everything to one person, somebody not mentioned in her present will.

Diane So now this original will stands? (*He nods*) And you inherit the lot?

Stephen Part of the estate goes to you and Ray, as her only relatives.

Diane H'm. Anyone convicted of her murder couldn't inherit.

Stephen Do you realize—the decision to change her will, cutting me out, does put me in jeopardy.

Diane The police know?

Stephen Sure, Corby told them. I'm sorry, Diane, I'm seeing stars. (*He puts his hand to his forehead*) We'll talk tomorrow. I'll drive you to the Mitre. (*He picks up her raincoat and arranges it round her shoulders*)

Diane We can't leave it, darling, we must find out who killed Norma.

Stephen Two lay people, battling in the dark. What hope do we have?

Diane You forget—I earn my living from murder. Except that in fiction you can provide more clues.

Stephen And the least suspicious person has always done it.

Diane Who's the least suspicious person in this Round Robin?

Stephen (*smiling*) You!

Diane (*turning into his arms; smiling*) Take me into custody, then.

Stephen Wish I could, but it's not wise, at this moment in time.

Diane Well, at least let me come over tomorrow evening and cook you a meal. Then we can decide what action to take.

Stephen What would your Inspector Quayle do?

Diane (*amused*) Oh, Quayle. (*Pause. Thoughtfully*) He'd set a trap.

Stephen What kind of trap?

Diane Well, we know someone gets in here to type those notes, so I suggest we watch the house. After dinner we'll leave the place in darkness and go out. Drive your car to a parking lot, than come back on foot.

Stephen I get you. I'll hide in the shrubbery across the road. I can watch the front door from there.

Diane And I'll be down the garden. Is there a shed or anything?

Stephen A summer-house.

Diane Good.

Stephen And if anyone shows up . . .

Diane We pounce!

They kiss lingeringly. Suddenly she draws back, glancing upstairs, frowning

Stephen What is it? (*Pause*) Darling . . .

Diane Listen—I thought I heard . . . oh, Stephen, it sounded like—footsteps upstairs. *Light* footsteps.

Stephen (*slowly*) It hasn't all been my imagination, has it?

He holds her close, protestingly, and she clings to him

Diane She hated us both. I never thought I'd be frightened of the dead, yet I am.

Stephen Come on, I'll get the car out.

Diane No. No, I can't leave you. (*She moves from his embrace and stands at the foot of the stairs*) I can't leave you alone—with *her*!

Stephen Diane, love, she can't hurt us any more. (*Softly*) Not any more.

Diane Can't she?

Stephen I shall probably sleep-walk again tonight. Round and round the house. I don't know why. It's as if in my subconscious I'm searching for something. Until I find it I can't rest.

Diane I'd like to—stay with you. May I?

Stephen Making quite sure I don't sleep-walk?

Diane nods. He smiles

Go up. I'll turn out the lights.

Diane mounts as far as the gallery, then turns and stops. Stephen switches out the lights. The room is illuminated only from the landing light above. He returns to the stairs, mounts them, then pauses on the gallery beside her

Stephen I've just remembered something. In your novel, *Hazard*, the victim was a woman, too.

Diane Can you recall who killed her?

Stephen (*slowly*) Yes . . . The husband's mistress.

They gaze at each other in silence, as—

the CURTAIN *falls*

SCENE 2

The same. The following night, midnight

The room is in darkness, except for a beam of torchlight. Ray is at the desk, using his torch as he searches amongst objects on the desk. Stephen enters from the hall in his raincoat and snaps on the lights by the archway. Ray, startled, swings round to face Stephen, then dives for the half-open garden door. Stephen rushes after him, catches him and they have a brief struggle

Stephen What the hell are you doing here?

Ray Leave me alone! Ow! Belt up! Let me go, damn you!

Stephen (*flinging Ray across the settee*) Now then, let's have an explanation. We've been watching the house from outside.

Ray Who's "we"? Not the fuzz?

Diane enters from the garden in her raincoat

Diane I saw someone creeping round the back; so it was *you*, Ray!

Ray Diane! It's great to see you again.

Stephen Skip the greetings. Turn out your pockets.

Ray I haven't stolen anything.

Stephen (*hauling Ray to his feet*) I said turn out . . .

Ray Okay, okay.

Ray turns out his pockets, putting a mingled collection on a table

Diane Car keys, coins, pen, book matches. What's that?

Stephen (*holding up a celluloid plectrum*) So this is how he breaks in.

Ray That's a plectrum. I use it for strumming my guitar.

Diane And for getting into people's houses.

Stephen Well, strum on the front door in future. Diane, you must be frozen. A drink?

Diane A cognac, please. (*She removes her raincoat*)

Ray I'll have a Scotch.

Stephen You'll have *nothing*!

Stephen flings his raincoat across a chair and goes to the drinks cabinet

And if you don't tell me why you broke in here tonight—I'll call the police.

Ray (*flopping on to the settee*) Isn't it bloody marvellous! I can't even make a social call . . .

Diane Social? At midnight?

Stephen Have you been typing notes?

Ray (*to Diane*) What's he on about?

Diane We caught you too early, didn't we? Another minute and you'd have been at that typewriter. (*She sits*)

Ray Why in hell should I do that? If I wanted anything typed I'd ask Sheila to do it, at her office.

Stephen Then what were you doing here? (*He takes a drink to Diane, then switches on the fire*)

Ray Nothing. Well, that is—nothing important.

Stephen We're waiting.

Ray Oh, I was looking for something.

Stephen Looking for what?

Diane You'd better tell us.

Ray "Us?" H'm, quite a romantic set-up. I didn't know Diane was living with you, Stephen. Quick work, one out, another in the bed. Cosy.

Stephen Another silly crack like that and I'll . . . (*He lifts a fist threateningly*)

Ray (*cowering back*) Just kidding.

Stephen Diane has a room at the Mitre. Now what were you searching for?

Ray Find out.

Stephen Right. (*He goes to the phone*)

Ray (*rising*) Not the police!

Diane You don't give us much option.

Stephen Condoning your behaviour could make us accessories after the fact.

Ray After the . . . you're joking.

Stephen Joking—about murder?

Ray You don't believe I killed . . . God, I know you have a low opinion of me . . .

Stephen It gets lower every minute.

Ray Why, for Christ's sake, should I want to kill her? She was a mean bitch, yes, but I had the measure of her. I could handle Norma.

Stephen Could you really? You had a very strong motive for murder.

Ray And what about *your* motive?

Stephen (*slowly replacing the receiver*) We were discussing *you*.

Ray Oh, sure. (*To Diane*) Know what they're saying about him at the university?

Diane I'm not interested.

Ray You should be. He's suspect No. 1.

Diane That's absurd.

Ray You know all about it, then? Where were *you* on the day Norma was murdered?

Diane On a plane, flying to Stockholm.

Ray And the night before, when the dryer was fixed?

Diane In London.

Ray Less than fifty miles from here. Time enough to drive down in the night—and leave without being seen.

Diane My car was in Cornwall.

Ray You could have hired one.

Stephen Diane had no motive.

Ray No? She was cut out of her grandad's will, wasn't she? And she was jealous as hell when you married Norma. She's got more motives than any of us. And if you weren't so bloody starry-eyed about her you'd see it.

Stephen That's enough!

Ray (*to Diane*) Can't deny it, can you? We've all known for years Norma got the man you fancied.

Diane Are you going to tell all this to the police?

Ray That depends.

Stephen Blackmail again.

Diane Suppose you tell us the truth, Ray. What were you searching for tonight?

Ray A button. It came off Sheila's jacket. We thought it might be here.

Diane Why were you worried about it?

Ray I didn't want the fuzz to start checking up on Sheila and me. Oh, I'm sick of everything. I've just had a flare up with Sheila's parents. They know she's in the club and they blamed *me*!

Stephen and Diane exchange smiles

Her old man said if I didn't fix the wedding soon, he'd report me to the Vice-Chancellor and have me sent down.

Stephen Don't worry. If they sent down every sexy student the college would be empty!

Ray I'm steamed off with it, anyway. I doubt if I'll get even a third class degree.

Stephen You would get an honours, if you worked. And that piece of paper would open all doors for you.

Ray I can't concentrate. Too much on my mind.

Stephen All you care about is getting your hands on that capital.

Ray 'Course, for Sheila's sake. But not enough to kill for it. Why don't you leave me alone and turn your sights on bigger game?

Diane Who?

Ray Well, for a start—Norma's boy friend.

Stephen Do you know who he is?

Ray No, but these book matches might give you a lead. (*He hands them to Stephen*)

Stephen (*reading the cover*) "The Green Flag Hotel, Cheltenham." When did you go there?

Ray I didn't. They—er—fell out of Norma's handbag.

Diane and Stephen look at him sceptically

Don't look like that, I only wanted my key back. I didn't nick any of her money.

Diane Only those book matches.

Ray I thought they might come in useful.

Stephen For blackmail?

Ray Well, she wouldn't let me have my legacy. I had to do something.

Stephen Like murder?

Ray Oh, try the flip side! (*He swings away*)

Stephen Why did you keep these matches?

Ray To strike a light! (*He sighs*) If you had your way I'd be all set for the Chamber of Horrors!

Stephen puts his half finished drink on the sofa table and takes a button from his pocket

Stephen Is this the button you were looking for?

Ray Yes. What a rotten, lousy trick! You had it all the time and you never said. (*He pockets the button*)

Stephen It slipped my memory.

Diane Ray, when did you take those matches from Norma's bag?

Ray Weeks ago, when I was living here.

Diane (*to Stephen*) I wonder if there's a link here?

Stephen With what? . . . Oh, the Green Flag Hotel and the missing week-end. (*He puts the matches on the mantelpiece*)

Diane Norma could have gone to Cheltenham after leaving my cottage.

Ray And met her lover boy there.

Stephen You knew about her affair, didn't you?

Ray What did you expect me to do—tell tales?

Diane Blackmail is worse.

Ray All right, so I'm a blackmailer and now you think I'm a murderer! Well, I don't care a damn what you say about me. But if anyone tries to stop me getting my legacy now, they'll be sorry. Bloody sorry!

Ray snatches up Stephen's drink, downs it fast, then marches out through the hall

Diane (*amused*) He's a stormy petrel these days. Do you really believe he's been typing these notes?
Stephen If he has, there might be one there now. (*He picks up the Plato*) Nothing there. Hey, look at this drawer. The lock's been broken! (*Examining a drawer*)
Diane Ray, I suppose. Anything missing?
Stephen I don't know. Norma kept all her private papers there.
Diane And he knew that?
Stephen I suppose so. After her death I used her key to open the drawer. I needed her deed box to hand over to the solicitors. But it wasn't there.
Diane I wonder—Ray said he was looking for a button, but that could have been an excuse. He might have been trying to find the deed box.
Stephen I can't imagine where Norma could have put it.
Diane Have you searched the place thoroughly?
Stephen Every corner I could think of.
Diane Are you sure? When Norma stayed with us as a child she used to hide her toys in the most unlikely places. May I look?

The telephone rings. Stephen answers it

After a moment, Diane hurries upstairs and off

Stephen (*into the phone*) Tudor . . . Sheila! . . . He left a few minutes ago . . . What? . . . Now take it easy, you can't walk the streets all night. Go home and . . . Stop being hysterical. Where are you speaking from? . . . Okay, I'll come and pick you up. Stay in the call-box, I'll be right there. (*He replaces the receiver and pulls on a raincoat, calling up the stairs*) Diane, I have to go out. Sheila's left home. She sounds quite desperate and hasn't anywhere to go. I'm fetching her in the car. Back soon.

Stephen exits through the hall.
There is a pause, then Diane appears on the stairs, carrying the deed box

Diane Found it! Guess where it was. The airing cupboard. (*She comes down, puzzled*) Stephen? (*Pause*) Darling, where are you? (*She goes and looks along the dining-room passage*) The deed box, I've found it. Stephen! (*She comes back into the room, glancing about her, then opens the lid of the box and looks inside*)

All the lights go out, the electric fire fades. A beam of moonlight across the room down stage is the only illumination

Oh, Stephen—the lights!

A figure, with a black academic gown concealing its face and head, comes from the hall and grabs Diane

Diane screams and the deed box falls with a clatter to the floor. Diane is flung face downwards into the pool of moonlight, where she lies still.

CURTAIN

SCENE 3

The same. Fifteen minutes later

When the CURTAIN *rises the lights are still out. Moonlight from the garden door faintly illumines Diane sprawled on the floor in the middle of the room. The deed box has gone. The book matches are still on the mantelpiece. The black academic gown is behind the sofa table*

Voices are heard in the hall, then Stephen and Sheila enter from it

Stephen Hallo, something wrong with the lights. Maybe it's a fuse.
Sheila Can't see a thing.
Stephen Wait there, I've got a torch. (*He takes a torch from his pocket*) Won't be a moment.

Stephen exits through the hall

Sheila looks about her nervously, wanders down stage, turns, and sees Diane. Gasping with terror, she backs away. The main lights go on

Stephen enters from the hall

Stephen The main switch had been turned off.
Sheila Look! (*She points to the floor*)
Stephen Good God! (*He kneels beside Diane and lifts her shoulders*) Help me to get her on to the settee, Sheila.

Between them they carry Diane to the settee. She opens her eyes weakly

Diane Oh, Stephen . . .
Stephen Get some water. (*He indicates the kitchen*)

Sheila runs out through the archway to the kitchen

Stephen Darling, what happened?
Diane I—I just remember everything—going dark.
Stephen You mean you blacked out. I'd never have left you if I'd known you weren't well.
Diane (*shakily*) You might have told me you were going.
Stephen I did. I called up the stairs.
Diane I didn't hear you.

Sheila enters with a glass of water, hurrying and slopping it over the carpet

Sheila Here you are.
Diane Thanks. (*She sips the water*)
Sheila Feeling any better?
Diane A little.
Stephen I'll call the doctor.
Diane Please, there's no need.
Stephen I think there is. (*He goes to phone, checks a number in the address book, and dials*)
Diane I'm all right, really.
Sheila You don't look it. When I saw you lying there I was scared. I thought you were—dead. Oh, I'm Sheila Hilton, by the way. I suppose you're Miss Diane Winslow. Professor Brent told me you were here. It was ever so good of him to come and fetch me.
Diane Fetch you—from where?
Sheila The phone-box. You see, I've left home. I went to Ray's digs but he wasn't there. I couldn't face my parents again. There's been such a barney. I felt like throwing myself in the river. Trouble is I can swim.
Stephen Number's engaged. I'll try again presently. (*He replaces the receiver*)
Diane Please don't bother. Your doctor won't like being called out this late.
Stephen Would you like a brandy?
Diane I'd rather have a coffee.
Sheila I'll make it.

Sheila bustles out to the kitchen

Stephen sits beside Diane on the settee and puts his arm round her

Stephen Now, darling . . .
Diane Can Sheila hear us from the kitchen?
Stephen I doubt it. Why?
Diane I found the deed box. It was in the airing cupboard.
Stephen Really? Strange hiding-place. Where did you put it?
Diane I had it in my hand when . . .
Stephen When you fainted?

Diane I didn't faint. All the lights went out. I thought they'd fused, but as I stood there in the darkness—I was attacked.

Stephen (*horrified*) You were—wha-at?

Diane A black shape came from the hall and grabbed me. I screamed and struggled and the box dropped out of my hands, then he struck me and I fell and—passed out.

Stephen That settles it. This is a matter for the police. (*Rising*) Who was it, did you see the face?

Diane No, just a figure. It was all over in a few moments. At first I thought it was—some kind of apparition.

Stephen This damned house!

Diane But the hands that gripped me were human. I'm sure it was a man.

Stephen What was he after?

Diane The deed box, I think. Can you see it anywhere?

Stephen (*looking for the box*) Not here.

Diane Then he must have stolen it.

Stephen Where did he come from?

Diane The hall.

Stephen Then he could have got in by the front door.

Diane But you'd only just gone out. There wasn't time.

Stephen My God, he could still be in the house!

Stephen goes out quickly towards the kitchen and dining-room, where Sheila is entering with a tray of coffee cups, spoons, and sugar bowl, which she puts on a table

Sheila Are you all right now, Miss Winslow?

Diane Yes, thanks.

Sheila Fainting makes you feel rotten, doesn't it? I fainted this morning, that's when Mum suspected. Are you in the club, too?

Diane (*amused*) No.

Sheila It's no fun, parents going on at you as if you'd done something criminal. Anyway, I'm still going to have a white wedding.

Diane Good for you.

Sheila But it'll have to be soon, or I won't look so nice in my wedding dress.

Stephen enters from the dining-room and goes to the stairs

Stephen Call your mother, Sheila, tell her where you are.

Sheila Not likely.

Stephen Let her know you'll be staying at the Mitre with Miss Winslow.

Stephen exits upstairs

Sheila Treating me like one of his students. Are you two keen on each other?

Diane (*rising*) We've been friends a long time. (*She picks up the book matches from the mantelpiece*) Ray was here tonight.

Sheila That must have been after he left our place.

Diane He said he came for your jacket button.

Sheila Oh, did he find it?

Diane Yes. (*Pause*) How well did you know my cousin Norma?

Sheila Hardly at all. Only met her twice. (*She looks at the bookcase*) You're quite famous, aren't you? I got a book of yours out of the library once.

Diane Enjoy it?

Sheila Yes, wasn't bad. Quite exciting. And I never guessed who'd done it.

Diane (*slowly*) Can you remember the title?

Sheila I dunno. It was—one word, I think.

Diane I often use one-word titles. Perhaps it was . . . *Hazard*?

Sheila *Hazard*. M'm, might be.

Diane That's the novel where the victim is killed—by a hair-dryer.

Sheila (*warily*) Oh! No, no, I didn't read that. Must have been some other book of yours.

Stephen comes downstairs. Seeing him, Sheila scuttles out to the kitchen

Stephen waits until Sheila has gone before he speaks

Stephen No sign of your attacker. You know, I've been thinking it over. If you're sure he came from the hall . . .

Diane He must have. (*Pointing*) I was standing right there.

Stephen Then he could have been hiding in the hall closet. That's where the main light switch is.

Stephen finds the gown lying behind the sofa table and picks it up

How the hell did this get here?

Diane Is it yours?

Stephen Yes, my gown.

Diane (*going to him*) That's what he had over his head. Where do you keep it?

Stephen It hangs in the hall closet. So he could have been hiding there even before I went out. But how did he get in?

Diane If he's the lover, Norma probably gave him a key.

Stephen And now he comes and goes as he please. (*Furiously*) In *my* house. He's the one typing these notes. My God, if I ever get my hands on him . . .

Diane Wait a moment: I remember now. I opened the lid of the deed box and saw a slip of paper on top of some documents. It was an I O U.

Stephen An I O U? Signed by . . . ?

Diane I didn't have a chance to see. The lights went out too quickly.

Stephen So someone gave Norma an I O U. Did you notice the amount?

Diane I think it was for two hundred—or two thousand.

Stephen (*snapping his fingers*) The missing two thousand pounds! She drew it out of the bank recently. I was never able to trace it.

Diane Why cash, why not a cheque?

Stephen Because she didn't want me to know about it, obviously. I'm going to call the police.

Diane No, don't.

Stephen Why not? You were attacked, you could have been killed.

Diane Please, darling.

Stephen He may come back. I'm not taking any more chances where you're concerned.

He starts to dial nine-nine-nine. Diane snatches the receiver away and slams it down

Diane We don't want the police yet.

Stephen I think we do.

Diane It's too risky. You're still under suspicion.

Stephen Then calling them proves my innocence.

Diane Does it? They mightn't see it that way. After all, could I swear it wasn't *you* who attacked me tonight?

Stephen Me?

Diane It would have been easy enough. You pretended to leave the house while I was upstairs, but instead you hid in the hall closet until I came down.

Stephen What possible motive . . .

Diane You didn't want me to see what was in the deed box. Then you left to pick up Sheila—to give yourself an alibi.

Stephen And the notes? I suppose I've been typing those to myself?

Diane Quite feasible. You had that accident, you were in hospital with concussion, you sleep-walk, and so you could be a little off centre.

Stephen Thank you.

Diane Look, in my profession I have a lot of dealings with the police. I know how their minds work. If I told them what's happened here to-night they'd probably arrest you and ask questions later.

Stephen What are you trying to do to me?

Sheila enters from the kitchen

Sheila I've plugged in the percolator. The coffee won't be long.

Stephen Call your parents.

Sheila They'll be in bed.

Stephen No, they won't. They'll be far too concerned about you. (*Glancing at Diane*) And if you don't ring they'll get on to the police, and we'll have them here on our doorstep.

Sheila (*turning towards the kitchen*) But I've got to see to the coffee.

Stephen *I'll* fix the coffee.

Stephen takes Sheila by the shoulders, turns her towards the phone, then exits to the kitchen

Sheila He's ever so bossy.
Diane But very kind. He did go out to pick you up, so the least you can do is ring your mother.
Sheila (*dialling*) They're always telling you to grow up and the next minute treating you like a kid.

Diane sits on the settee and studies the book matches

(*Into the phone*) Mum. I'm round at Professor Brent's place . . . No, they're going to fix me up a room at the Mitre . . . Well, Dad was dead rotten to Ray. It wasn't all Ray's fault. Takes two, you know . . . Oh, Mum, don't be so old-fashioned, *every*body does it! . . . I'll ring you again sometime. 'Bye. (*She replaces the receiver*) Parents!
Diane Wait till you're one yourself.
Sheila Won't have to wait long. Mine are the end. The names Dad called Ray, anyone'd think he'd done a murder! (*She stops, putting her hand to her mouth nervously*)
Diane (*rising*) Sheila, you were using the hair-dryer the evening before my cousin died, weren't you?
Sheila Wish I hadn't now. They blew that up at the inquest.
Diane Do you think her death was an accident?
Sheila We all did at first. But now, with the police asking questions and everything—well, I don't know *what* to think. I wish Ray and I could go away somewhere—you know, elope.
Diane Have you any idea who's responsible?
Sheila If I had I'd tell the police, wouldn't I?
Diane Not if it happened to be someone you were—very fond of.
Sheila Depends.
Diane Your father has an electrical shop, I understand.
Sheila Yep. High Street. Business isn't so good and that makes him irritable.
Diane Have you ever served behind the counter?
Sheila Sometimes, on a Saturday.
Diane So you know something about electricity.
Sheila A bit. (*Quickly*) Not much.
Diane Still, you'd know if you'd damaged a hair-dryer and made it unsafe to use?
Sheila I never said I damaged it. (*She looks worried now*)
Diane It might help Ray, if you told the truth.
Sheila He isn't mixed up in any of this.
Diane The police may think he is. My cousin's death was very convenient for Ray—*and for you.*
Sheila (*rushing at Diane*) Ray didn't kill her, he didn't, he didn't! You're not to say he did, you're not to!
Diane (*catching Sheila's hands*) Now calm down, Sheila, and listen. Inspector Neville may want to see you. He's bound to ask if you damaged the dryer. What will you tell him? (*Gently*) It's true, isn't it? You did damage it?
Sheila No! (*She pulls away*) Well . . . not really. I mean, what I did couldn't have made any difference.

Diane What *did* you do?

Sheila I—well, I put it down on that table—and it fell on the floor. It got chipped, that's all. I swear that's all.

Diane Did you tell them that at the inquest?

Sheila No.

Diane Why not?

Sheila I was scared. They kept asking questions and I got in a flap. But I never told any lies. (*Defiantly, shouting tearfully*) I don't want to be sent to prison for purgatory! (*She flops into a chair*)

Diane (*smiling*) Why were you scared, Sheila? Was it for Ray?

Sheila Of course. Who else?

Diane Because he hadn't admitted he'd come back that night—for your jacket?

Sheila Well, it would have looked bad, wouldn't it?

Diane For him, Sheila? Or for you?

Stephen enters with a coffee-pot and milk

Stephen Have you called your mother, Sheila?

Diane Yes, she has.

Stephen Good girl. You like your coffee white, don't you, Diane?

Diane Please.

Stephen And you, Sheila?

Sheila I don't want any coffee, thanks. I think I'll go.

Stephen I thought you were going to stay at the Mitre with Diane.

Sheila I'm not sure I want to now. She makes me feel guilty, just 'cos I . . . (*She breaks off*)

Stephen Because you what?

Sheila Dropped the dryer and a bit got chipped off.

Stephen So you *did* damage it!

Sheila (*tearfully*) Oh, don't *you* start! If you let on to Ray that I told you he'll never speak to me again. (*She runs to the hall archway, then turns, shouting*) And I don't want to be an unmarried mother!

Sheila runs off through the hall

Diane So now we know. Sheila dropped the dryer and chipped it.

Stephen That wouldn't make it lethal.

Diane No, but Ray did come back later that night . . .

Stephen To fetch the jacket, he said.

Diane And then he saw the dryer again and that could have inspired him. Does he know much about electrical gadgets?

Stephen In an amateur way, yes. When he lived here he was always experimenting. One night he blew all the fuses and I had to grope around in the hall closet to find the fuse box. On that occasion he'd been tinkering with the hi-fi equipment.

Diane So he's a boy who likes to meddle. I wonder—a way to settle his score with Norma, perhaps?

Stephen Oh, come on, Ray's not the type.

Diane You're biased in his favour, darling. Little boys grow up, and he and Sheila had a load of worry. Of course, it could have been a joint effort. A quick despatch and no more money problems.

Stephen If the girl had been involved, I guess she wouldn't have owned up to chipping the dryer.

Diane It could be her alibi, making it appear to be an accident.

Stephen That's possible.

Diane And she is very, very frightened. But I mustn't jump to conclusions. The first law of detective fiction is: if it looks easy, discard it. So for the time being I'll keep an open mind.

Stephen Someone's entering this house quite freely, coming and going as they please. So tomorrow I'll change the lock on the front door and make sure all the other doors and windows are bolted.

Diane (*holding up the book matches*) I believe there's a clue here, darling, and I'd like to follow it up. May I borrow Norma's car tomorrow?

Stephen Sure, but why do you want it?

Diane I'm going to drive over to Cheltenham.

Stephen To the Green Flag Hotel?

Diane Right. I'll make a few discreet inquiries and see what I come up with.

Stephen What do you think they can tell you?

Diane I'm not sure yet. But they may recall a couple booking in for the week-end last August.

Stephen I get it.

Diane I'll say I'm trying to trace my cousin, but as she recently married I don't know her new name. My resemblance to Norma might jog their memories.

Stephen You'll take care, won't you?

Diane Don't worry, darling.

Stephen I could cancel my tutorials tomorrow and come with you.

Diane There's no need. Now would it be possible to have a little sherry party here tomorrow evening?

Stephen A sherry party?

Diane Just for a few select people. The ones who were here the night before Norma—died.

Stephen Sure, I'll arrange it. Will you be back in time?

Diane Of course. I want to meet your friends.

Stephen (*slowly, with an ironic inflection*) My friends . . . or my enemies?

CURTAIN

SCENE 4

The same. The following evening

When the CURTAIN *rises the lights are on, the window curtains open. Moonlight streams in, making a cross-beam in the middle of the room. There is now a low red bulb in the desk lamp, though this is not switched on until later*

Cliff is seated in a chair, Joan on the settee. They both have drinks, and Stephen is moving to them to top up their glasses. Joan makes a "no more for me" gesture by covering the rim, but Cliff allows his glass to be refilled

Cliff The market's very healthy now, you should get a good price. Of course, there's nothing like selling by auction, only that takes time.

Stephen I want a quick sale.

Joan Where will you live after you've sold the house?

Stephen The States. I'll take up the lectureship I was offered.

Cliff Completely fresh start, eh? Good idea.

Joan I only hope our new neighbours will be as friendly as you and—and Norma.

Stephen puts a hand to his head

Joan Oh, sorry, I shouldn't have mentioned her.

Stephen It's all right. I get a lot of headaches and I don't sleep too well. Even my memory's faulty. I had a letter to write today and I couldn't remember the date.

Cliff The twenty-fourth.

Joan Is it, dear? I thought it was the twenty-fifth.

There is a knock on the front door

Stephen Excuse me.

Stephen exits to the hall

Cliff goes to the window and looks out

Joan Who is it?

Cliff Tony Marshall. Bought himself a new car, by the look of it. Very flash.

Joan Stephen's not wasting any time, is he? Selling up and going back to America. The police may think he's running away.

There is a murmur of voices in the hall, then Stephen enters with Tony

Tony We don't want to spend too much on scenery, and I wondered if you had any suggestions?

Stephen A simple framework's best in classical plays. You can do a lot with a flight of steps and a few Doric columns.

Cliff (*lightly*) You know, Pearl and Dean.

They all smile politely

Stephen We'll discuss it more fully later on. (*Going to the cabinet*) Park yourself, Tony. What'll you drink?

Tony Scotch, neat, please. (*He sits*)

Stephen (*meaningly*) Neat? Sure. (*He pours a drink*)

Tony (*to Joan and Cliff*) Nice to see you both again.

Cliff Oh, Marshall, I . . .

Tony Yes, yes, I've put you on the *short* list.

Cliff Good.

Tony But it's rather a *long* list.

Cliff sighs. Stephen smiles and takes a drink to Tony

Joan Stephen's been telling us he's going to put the house on the market. He wants a quick sale.

Tony Really? You're not leaving us altogether?

Stephen Yes, if all goes well.

Tony You can't go yet, surely. The police . . .

Stephen What *about* the police?

Tony Still making inquiries, aren't they?

Stephen I've helped them all I can.

Cliff Oh, you know the way they drag things on.

Stephen (*looking at his watch*) Ray and Sheila are late.

Joan Are they coming round?

Stephen I hope so. Oh, excuse me. I'll get some ice.

Stephen exits to the kitchen

Joan He's been very odd lately.

Cliff It's the strain of everything.

Tony Funny, it's the same set-up.

Cliff How do you mean?

Tony After the inquest—don't you remember? We were all here that day. Why has he asked the five of us round again?

Cliff Does there have to be a reason? We're his friends.

Stephen enters with the ice bowl

There is a knock on the front door. Stephen puts the bowl on the cabinet

Stephen That'll be the kids now. Help yourselves to ice, if you need it.

Stephen exits to the hall

Tony rises and passes round the ice bowl

Joan The police were here this afternoon.

Tony Really? Again?

Joan I was weeding my front lawn when they drove up. They stayed quite a time.

Cliff Poor old Stephen. They don't give him much peace, do they? Questions, questions. He must be dizzy with all their interrogations.

Joan I was very worried. I was afraid they'd come to arrest him.

Stephen (*off*) Go along in, I'll hang up your things. Help yourselves to drinks.

Ray and Sheila enter

Ray (*to Sheila, as they come in*) Stephen must be losing his memory. Fancy asking us today's date.
Sheila Oh, hallo, everyone. Didn't know it was going to be a party.
Ray Salaams. (*He bows, touches both hands to his brow, then pours drinks for Sheila and himself*)
Joan How are you, Sheila?
Sheila Fine.
Joan The last time we met you were rather depressed.
Ray (*putting his arm round Sheila*) Today she's singing. We've just got engaged.

Sheila proudly displays her ring

Cliff Congratulations.
Tony Best of luck.
Joan When's the wedding?
Sheila Soon as possible.

Stephen enters from the hall

Tony Look, Stephen, I don't want to bore these people with my production problems. Perhaps we could get together another time to talk about the show. I'll push off now, if you don't mind.
Stephen Don't go, Tony, I need your help.
Tony In what way?
Stephen Could we rearrange the furniture? Come on, Ray, lend a hand. Swing the settee round to face the desk.
Ray Oh, not home movies!

They rearrange the furniture, with the sofa and chairs facing the desk

Joan And I'd just got comfortable. I hope you're not going to show any films of Norma. It would only upset you, Stephen, and nothing can be gained.
Cliff Probably slides of his American trip.
Tony All right, is this how you want it?
Stephen Yes, that's okay.
Cliff All set, then. Where's the screen?

They settle down—Joan, Sheila and Ray on the settee, Cliff and Tony on chairs. Stephen remains standing

Stephen No screen, no movies. I want to try an experiment. You see, certain incidents have been occurring in this house lately, incidents I've found very disturbing. (*Pause*) I've been receiving notes—signed "Norma".

Cliff *What* did you say?

Tony You mean someone sent you letters, pretending they're from . . .

Stephen They didn't come through the post. They were typed right here—on this machine—and left in my copy of Plato's *Republic*. (*He picks up the Plato*)

Ray Just like she used to do. (*To Sheila*) Remember, I showed you . . . (*He breaks off, embarrassed*)

Tony If this is a joke I find it in poor taste.

Stephen It's no joke, it's for real.

Joan Quite true. I was here when Stephen found one of the notes, and I remember thinking then . . .

Cliff You didn't tell *me*.

Joan Well, he asked me not to mention it to anyone.

Cliff I'm not "anyone".

Tony What do the notes say?

Stephen The first one—that Norma would come back.

Tony You don't really believe . . .

Ray Oh, come on, she's dead. She couldn't have typed . . .

Sheila She might have used someone as a medium. I saw it in a play on telly once. The murderer was controlled by the wife he'd killed . . .

Stephen You think it's possible *I'm* being used, my subconscious mind taken over? (*He looks around him*) On the other hand, someone could have got in here—and typed the notes while I was out or in bed asleep.

Ray Why, for God's sake?

Stephen Who knows? To drive me out of my mind, maybe, hoping I'll then confess to a crime I didn't commit.

Joan All this talk about crime and murder. I still believe it was an accident with the hair-dryer.

Stephen Inspector Neville wouldn't agree. He was here this afternoon.

Joan Yes, I saw the police car.

Stephen There's no doubt at all it was murder. And now the killer is gunning for *me*. (*Pause*) I wonder who hates me so much?

Joan Nobody hates you.

Cliff Of course they don't.

Tony You're very popular—everywhere.

Stephen Yet I have a mysterious enemy, pushing me towards the brink. You all know I had a car accident in New York. Now I keep having nightmares. And running through them I hear music, the same music Norma was playing the day she died. This record.

Stephen puts on a record. Soft music is heard. He takes a photograph from the mantelpiece, puts it on the desk and switches on the desk lamp, which glows red

I want you to help me in this. Will you all sit perfectly still and concentrate on Norma's photograph?

Cliff Now wait a minute . . .

Stephen I want you to fix your minds on her, think of her as you knew her in life. That way we may be able to build up enough power—for her to come back.

Joan You're not going to hold a seance?

Tony What a morbid idea. You can't believe—a man of your intelligence . . .

Stephen Nobody believes, until it happens to them. Do you want to help me or don't you?

Joan Of course, but not in this way. (*Rising*) I think we should all go. Come on, Cliff.

Stephen Not yet, Joan. I have to know the truth. Who killed my wife?

Sheila How can a seance tell you? I mean, whatever happens that wouldn't be proof.

Ray 'Course it wouldn't.

Stephen Look, if Norma comes back and accuses me of her murder, I promise you I'll give myself up to the police.

Joan Don't do this, please. After all you've been through, the shock could . . .

Stephen The shock could—unbalance me?

Joan Don't let him do it, Cliff. Stop him!

Cliff Stephen, you *have* been under a strain. It's not wise.

Tony I don't think we should dabble in these things. It's all right as a game, but he's taking it seriously.

Stephen Don't you want to know if I'm guilty?

Tony (*rising*) I'm damned if I'll take part in any supernatural stunt at Norma's expense. We should honour her memory. I liked and admired her.

Stephen Yes, I know you did.

They face each other, Tony unsure of the implication. He suddenly turns and starts to walk to the hall archway

If you quit now, Tony, I'll draw my own conclusions.

Tony What the hell do you mean by that?

Ray He means either you're scared—or you've got something to hide.

Tony You insolent little bastard!

Tony glares at Ray, then sits again near Sheila

Stephen Now if you're all ready . . .

Sheila (*clutching Ray*) Oh, Ray, I'm frightened.

Ray It's all right, sweetie, I'm here.

Ray blows out his cheeks nervously. Stephen switches off the main lights. A red glow illumines the typewriter and photograph. Moonlight faintly lights the centre of the room. Stephen sits at the desk, slips some paper into the typewriter, and rests his fingers on the keys

Stephen Please don't move, anyone. It's essential that we all remain still and calm.

Sheila Calm, he says!

Tony (*after a pause*) We could sit here like this for hours. It's a sheer waste of time.

Sheila (*shivering*) Nothing's really going to happen, is it, Ray? I mean, it's a lot of . . .

Ray 'Sssh!

Joan It's turned very cold.

Tony They say the temperature drops—when there are psychic elements around.

Cliff You're not starting to believe this, surely?

Stephen If anything unusual occurs, I want you all to stay silent, please.

Silence. Stephen's hands are poised over the keys. Slowly he begins to type

Sheila He did type those notes to himself, he did!

Ray 'Sh, quiet!

They all sit tensely watching Stephen

Then a figure, wearing the white death clothes of Norma, appears from the bookcase. The back of her gown is black, so that she is unseen until she turns to face front. She moves slowly into the moonlight

Sheila screams and clutches Ray

The figure turns and vanishes

Sheila screams again, hysterically, jumps up, and rushes for the archway. Ray dives after her and catches her in his arms

Ray It's all right, love, it's all right.

Tony switches on the lights, then stops the record. Stephen stops typing and slumps over the keys like a man in a trance

Joan It was Norma! (*She buries her face in her hands*) Oh God, it was Norma!

Cliff She's dead.

Sheila It *was* her, it was! She was wearing those clothes that morning. I saw her!

Joan Stephen . . . (*Going to him*) Stephen . . .

Stephen sits absolutely still, almost as though dead. Then he swivels round to face them

Stephen What happened?

Sheila Your wife—she appeared! She appeared just as if she were still alive!

Stephen Materialised?

Tony You didn't see anything?

Stephen slowly rises, then turns, takes the paper out of the machine and scans it

Cliff Well, what does it say?
Ray Does she accuse you, Stephen?
Tony Perhaps he'd rather not answer that.
Joan I don't think he *should* read us the note—not if it incriminates him.
Cliff Does it, Stephen?

Stephen looks from one to the other and remains silent. Tony impatiently makes for the hall archway

Tony Oh, well, if you won't say, I'm going.
Stephen Hang on, Tony. Aren't you curious?
Tony Of course I damn well am. But if you won't even show us the note.
Ray Come on, does it tell you who killed Norma?
Stephen (*slowly deliberately*) It tells me—all I need to know.

There is a knock on the garden door. Stephen opens it and speaks off

Oh, hallo, glad you were able to join the party. Come in.

Diane enters from the garden, hatless, wearing a suit and carrying a week-end case

Diane Good evening.

They all stare at her, transfixed

Stephen May I introduce Norma's cousin, Miss Diane Winslow. Mr and Mrs Prior, Mr Tony Marshall. And of course you know Ray and Sheila.
Tony You're the image of Norma.
Diane So I've been told. (*She puts her case on the desk, then turns to face them*)
Stephen Diane, shortly before you arrived, we held a little seance here. I went into a trance and was influenced to write a note. Naturally, everyone wants to hear what's in it. Tony, perhaps you'd like to read it out to us?

Stephen hands the note to Tony, who scans it, frowning, then glances around at all of them

Ray Well, come on, what's it say?
Tony It's signed "Norma", and it reads: "The person who killed me is in this room *now*!"

Everyone reacts

Cliff And I think we all know who that is.
Ray All right, tell us.
Cliff I have no proof.
Stephen Okay, let's wait till we *get* proof. Diane, I think my guests would be interested to hear what happened to you in this room last night.
Diane I was attacked.

The others gasp in shocked reaction

It was when I was alone here. Someone must have been hiding in the
hall closet. All the lights went out and this character came at me.

Tony Did you see who it was?

Diane No. It happened not long after you'd left, Ray. That's if you did
leave.

Ray Don't turn your bloody guns on *me*! Why should I want to attack
you?

Joan Why should *anyone* want to attack you?

Diane To steal Norma's deed box. I'd just opened it and found an I O U
inside. For two thousand pounds.

Ray The vanished two thousand quid.

Tony A quick reflex, Ray.

Ray Signed by?

Diane I hadn't time to see.

Tony Well, who's been flashing money about lately?

Cliff (*looking at Tony*) Someone was able to buy an expensive new car.

Tony What are you insinuating?

Ray I guess he's wondering how you found the cash for it. The police
might wonder, too.

Tony Speaking of the police, tell your uncle why *you* had a visit from them.

Ray turns away, looking guilty

Stephen Did you, Ray?

Tony It was before Norma died . . .

Ray You bloody snooper!

Stephen What did the police want?

Ray That's *my* business.

Tony As he's reluctant to tell you, *I* will.

Sheila We've paid up. Everything's all right now. Honest.

Tony Ray wanted to raise the deposit for his present car, so he sold his
motor bike—while it was still on hire purchase.

Joan And didn't keep up the payments? That's criminal, Ray.

Tony Which he knew. Norma wouldn't help him and he had to make a
quick settlement—or go to jail. Once she was dead, of course——

Sheila He didn't kill her, he didn't!

Tony —the bank knew Ray's legacy would come to him soon, so they
advanced him all he needed.

Cliff Been checking up on him, have you, Marshall?

Tony One hears things—at the club.

Ray Leave me alone, blast you!

Diane Sheila, will you do something for me?

Sheila What?

Diane opens her case, takes out a dryer, and goes to Sheila

Diane Will you hold this?

Sheila (*backing away to the garden door*) No! I didn't do anything. You've
got to believe me. It wasn't my fault!

Diane Please hold it, Sheila.

Trembling, Sheila takes the dryer

Diane This is the hair-dryer you used the night before Norma died, isn't it? The dryer you damaged?

Joan Damaged?

Ray What are you trying to do—scare Sheila?

Diane She didn't tell the whole truth at the inquest.

Sheila I was confused, I didn't want to say . . .

Diane You didn't want to say that the dryer they showed you, the dryer that killed Norma, was *not* the one you had taken from upstairs that night?

Sheila I wasn't sure. (*Sobbing*) Honestly, I wasn't sure.

Diane But you knew the one in the coroner's court wasn't chipped, didn't you?

Sheila nods miserably

Ray Why the hell didn't you say so at the inquest?

Sheila (*going to Ray*) I was worried for *you*. I knew you'd come back here for my jacket that night and I thought . . .

Ray You didn't imagine I'd got busy on the dryer?

Sheila No, but I was afraid the police might think so.

Tony They would, too. So Sheila damaged the dryer and Ray came back to see if he could mend it. Instead he got the wires crossed . . .

Cliff And Norma died as a result.

Ray I didn't touch the bloody dryer! Why do you all pick on *me*?

Ray takes the dryer from Sheila and opens Diane's case to put it back. Then he sees the white housecoat and turban and lifts them out, holding them up

So it was *you*, Diane! I might have guessed.

Sheila But she came through the bookcase.

Stephen Sure.

At the bookcase he touches a concealed spring and the centre of the bookcase opens like a door, revealing a dim room with a drawing board visible

Cliff Good God! Where does it lead to? A passage between the two cottages?

Diane No, into an office.

Stephen *Your* office, Cliff.

Cliff Well, I'm damned!

Joan Why didn't you tell us about it?

Stephen I didn't know myself until today. I knew someone had been getting in, so I had the locks changed, yet there was another note waiting for me when I got home.

Joan But you've just shown us you were typing those notes yourself.

Ray He was only stringing us along. A phoney seance and a phoney apparition.

Stephen True. I wanted your reactions.

Tony How did you find out there was a hidden door?

Stephen I went to the university library and looked up an old manual. In it I came across the original plans of this building. They showed that a door connected this room to one on the other side.

Cliff How strange. I didn't find it when I was doing the conversion.

Joan Does this mean someone's been using *our* house to get in here?

Cliff (*looking at Tony*) That's obvious.

Tony Don't look at *me*. Housebreaking isn't one of *my* hobbies.

Diane But it is one of *yours*, isn't it, Ray?

Ray I didn't know about that door. In any case . . .

Diane We know. You have your own methods.

Cliff Has he indeed?

Stephen (*taking a note from his pocket*) This is the note I found today. It's signed "Norma", as usual, and it's dated. I've asked everyone the date —oh, everyone except you, Tony. Do you know what it is?

Tony The twenty-fifth, of course.

Stephen That's right. But Cliff was the only one who thought it was—the twenty-fourth.

Cliff Anyone can get a date wrong.

Stephen I deliberately left yesterday's date on my desk calendar.

Ray A trap!

Stephen Yes. I guessed someone would fall into it. And they did. Well, Cliff, why did you type those notes?

Cliff Me? I—I didn't type any . . .

Stephen (*bearing down on him*) You'd better tell us.

Cliff Well—well, I—I had to do something. You were getting away with murder!

Diane Oh, come on! You were trying to unhinge Stephen's mind, con him into imagining he'd walked in his sleep and . . .

Cliff (*roaring*) He killed Norma, I know he did! I heard them through the wall. They were quarrelling violently. He was threatening her. I was half inclined to burst in here and . . .

Diane (*pointing to the door*) Through that hidden door?

Cliff (*looking round desperately*) All right, so I did know about it. I meant to board it up some time.

Ray Cobblers! You used it to get in here and bash away at that typewriter.

Tony Stephen, why were you quarrelling with Norma?

Stephen I'd found out she had a lover. I asked her to give him up. She refused.

Tony Did she tell you his name?

Stephen No, Tony, she didn't.

Diane So we decided to find out. This morning I drove to Cheltenham and called at the Green Flag Hotel.

Ray The book matches place!

Diane Yes. The receptionist remembered a couple staying there for a weekend in August. The wife, she said, looked very much like me. They signed in as Mr and Mrs Jackson.

Tony Who the hell is Jackson?

Ray Perhaps you can tell us, Tony?

Tony How the blazes should *I* know?

Ray (*cheekily*) Thought he might be a member of your golf club.

Diane Mr Jackson—though that wasn't his real name—returned to the hotel just over a week ago and said his "wife" would be joining him. But she never arrived. And we all know why.

Ray Norma had planned to clear out and meet lover boy at the hotel?

Diane Yes, I spoke to every member of the staff. Their descriptions were pretty vague where the man was concerned, but finally the hall porter remembered one thing . . .

Tony Well?

Diane Mr Jackson came in a van. On the side it said: "Property Conversions Limited."

They all look at Cliff. Joan's face reveals shocked astonishment

Joan Oh, no! Not Cliff.

Stephen (*going to Cliff*) That secret door was very convenient for you, wasn't it? A way for lovers to meet without being seen by the neighbours. It was also very simple for you to get in here that night—and tamper with the hair-dryer.

Cliff Christ, are you mad? I had no reason to kill Norma.

Diane It was you who attacked me—to get that deed box. Norma had lent you two thousand pounds, and you didn't want anyone to see the I O U.

Stephen You must have been here, searching for the box, when Ray let himself in. No time for you to escape through the bookcase door, so you hid in the hall closet.

Diane And when I was alone, and you heard me call out to Stephen that I'd found the deed box, you threw the main switch, plunging the house into darkness, and came at me.

Cliff What a vivid imagination.

Stephen Do you deny having an affair with my wife?

Tony How can he deny it now?

Cliff All right, I loved her.

Joan turns away, distressed

We'd planned to go away together. She asked me to meet her in Cheltenham and I went there and waited. If I'd killed her I'd hardly have gone to the Green Flag Hotel and hung about there for hours.

Ray You might have done—to give yourself an alibi.

Cliff Don't be bloody wet!

Stephen And the two thousand pounds?

Cliff Norma asked me to invest it for her—in a property deal. We were going into partnership in a new business venture. (*To Stephen*) But you wrecked all that. She told you she was going to change her will, cutting you out . . .

Stephen And leaving all her money to *you*?

Cliff Yes. So you had to act fast. You wanted to make damned sure I never got Norma *or* her money. (*To the others*) That's why he murdered her, cynically, ruthlessly, before the will could be changed.

Stephen listens impassively

Nobody had more opportunity—or more motive for rigging that hair-dryer. My God, you only have to look at him to see how bloody guilty he is!

Diane (*to Cliff*) Why didn't you tell the police all this? Why write malicious notes? Or was that part of your twisted mentality? The satisfaction of watching Stephen go slowly out of his mind?

Cliff He deserved to suffer for the way he treated Norma. Well, now you all know the truth.

Diane Do we? (*Taking the dryer from her case*) Sheila, take another look at this dryer. (*She hands the dryer to Sheila*) Could you swear it's the one you used?

Sheila Yes. There's the chip I made when I dropped it. I didn't mean to drop it, only it slipped . . .

Stephen Then the dryer that killed Norma, the one shown at the inquest, whom does that belong to?

Stephen looks at each person in turn, then goes to Joan

To *you*, doesn't it, Joan?

Joan No, it doesn't. What are you talking about?

Stephen Cliff got two identical dryers through the trade, gave one to you, and sold the other to Norma.

Joan That's right. Mine is next door.

Stephen No. Yours is in the hands of the police. Norma wasn't killed with her own dryer—but with *yours*, Joan!

Everyone reacts. Joan is petrified

You found out Cliff was having an affair with Norma—and you were determined to put a stop to it.

Diane About the same time that you discovered the hidden door between the two cottages.

Stephen Someone sent me an anonymous cable when I was in New York. *Only Norma* knew I was staying at the Manhattan Hotel. Did she tell you, Joan?

Joan No! Anyway, how could I have sent a cable? I haven't been to London for months.

Stephen I didn't say it had come from *London*.

Joan (*confused*) Oh, I—I thought . . . Well, I—I did it for *your* sake as well as mine. I only wanted to break up the affair—and save my marriage.

Stephen And you figured the best way to do that was—to murder my wife?

Joan (*backing away*) No. How could I? I don't know a thing about electricity. I can't even mend a fuse.

Diane The details were all in my novel, *Hazard.* I gave Norma a copy. Did she lend it to you?

Joan No!

Stephen Cliff, did *you* borrow it?

Cliff No, I damn well didn't!

Diane takes a book from her case and holds it up

Diane But I found it next door.

Cliff (*wildly*) You're lying! I returned . . . (*He stops abruptly*)

Stephen (*slowly*) You returned the book, Cliff, after you'd read it—and taken down all the relevant details.

Cliff I didn't read it. Joan did.

Joan You bastard! Trying to swing this on *me*!

Cliff (*going to the bookcase door*) I'm getting out of here.

Joan That's right, run away, let everyone think *I* killed her. (*To the others*) If it hadn't been for Cliff, she'd be alive today.

Cliff (*turning*) You're jealous, jealous because I loved Norma.

Joan (*bitterly*) Loved her! All you cared about was her money! (*To the others*) He was facing bankruptcy, the creditors were closing in—that's why he was willing to run away with Norma. To escape his debts. As for that bitch, she didn't care a damn whose life she wrecked, so long as she got what she wanted. She was greedy and selfish and I hated her. God, how I hated her!

Cliff Shut up, you fool!

Joan Why should I? Let them know the truth about that scheming whore!

Tony And what *is* the truth?

Joan She rang Cliff the night before she died. He thought I was in the *bath*, but I wasn't. I listened-in on my bedroom extension. She asked him to go away with her the next day. He told her I'd never divorce him, and Norma said: (*Pause*) "Well, do as I suggested!" Then Cliff answered: "You mean fix it to get rid of Joan?" (*Hysterically*) Don't you see now? They'd planned it all—planned to get rid of *me*!

Cliff She's out of her mind!

Stephen What happened then, Joan?

Joan I was in bed, pretending to be asleep, when Cliff came in. He took the dryer from my dressing-table and I lay there, trembling, until he brought it back. I guessed then he'd "fixed it", as Norma had told him to do.

Diane So later that night you came in here—through that hidden door— *and switched over the two dryers!*

Joan (*sobbing*) I only gave Norma what she meant *me* to have! (*She moves to the bookcase, then turns to face them all*) Don't you understand? I had to do it—in self-defence!

Distressed, Joan exits through the bookcase door. Cliff follows her out. The door closes

Ray You're not letting them get away with it?

Stephen No. Inspector Neville came this afternoon and arranged concealed microphones around this room.

Ray Well, I'm damned!

Stephen The mikes are linked by short wave radio to police headquarters.

Sheila You mean they've heard everything we said here this evening?

Diane Yes. And they'll have tape-recorded it.

Tony Then that means they'll be round here soon—to make a double arrest next door.

Ray and Sheila turn to the window to look out, arms around each other. Stephen and Diane stand close to each other

Diane How could they have gone on living together?

Stephen No option. Each knew the other was—a party to murder.

Diane But then so was Norma.

Stephen Ye-es. (*Thoughtfully, looking front*) She was, in effect—*her own executioner!*

CURTAIN

FURNITURE AND PROPERTY LIST

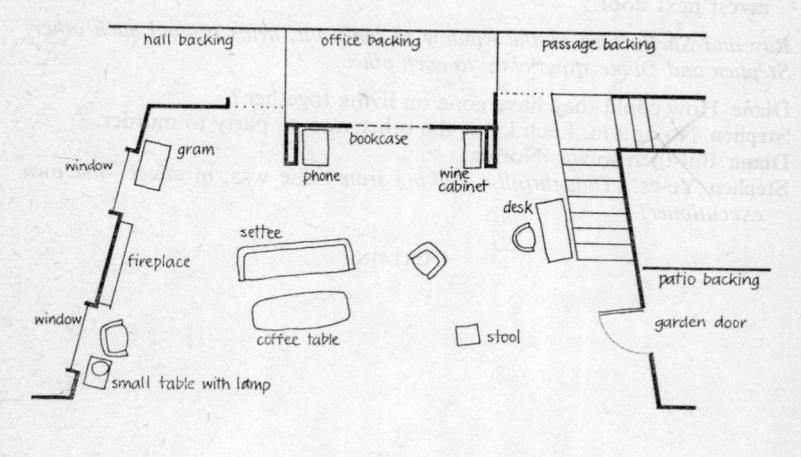

ACT I

SCENE 1

On stage: Settee. *On it:* cushions
2 armchairs
Stool
Coffee-table. *On it:* ashtray
Desk. *On it:* lamp, portable typewriter, paper, books including Plato's *Republic* with note tucked inside, address pad, pens, letters in envelopes. *In drawers:* papers, deed box. *Under it:* waste-paper basket
Desk chair
Gramophone and records
Drinks cabinet. *On it:* gin, vodka, sherry, tomato juice, bitter lemon, whisky, glasses, soda water, bottle opener
Occasional table (*above settee*) *On it:* telephone, pad, pencil
High bookcase with books and secret door
Occasional table (*below fire*) *On it:* lamp
Drawing-board (*behind bookcase door*)
On walls: various pictures
On mantelpiece: Norma's photograph, cigarette box, lighter, ashtray
Below fire: practical plug for hair-dryer
Carpet
Window curtains

Off stage: Celluloid plectrum (**Ray**)
              White portable hair-dryer (**Sheila**)
              Suitcase (**Stephen**)
              Briefcase with papers and wrapped gift (**Stephen**)
              Cable (**Stephen**)
              Torch (**Ray**)

SCENE 2

Strike: Dirty glasses
             Sheila's jacket

Set: Newspaper on settee

Off stage: Cup of coffee (**Stephen**)

SCENE 3

Strike: Newspaper
             Hair-dryer

Set: Plato's *Republic* on desk with other books, and note inserted in it

Off stage: Tray with 2 cups, saucers, spoons, sugar bowl, milk jug, hot-water
                jug, teapot
             2 cups, saucers, spoons (**Joan**)

ACT II

SCENE 1

Strike: Dirty glasses

SCENE 2

Strike: Dirty glasses

Off stage: Torch (**Ray**)
             Button (**Stephen**)
             Deed box (**Diane**) from Act I

Personal: **Ray:** various objects in pockets including celluloid plectrum, book
             matches

SCENE 3

Strike: Deed box

Off stage: Torch **(Stephen)**
Glass of water **(Sheila)**
Tray with 3 coffee cups, saucers, spoons, sugar bowl **(Sheila)**
Coffee-pot and milk jug **(Stephen)**

SCENE 4

Strike: Coffee things
Glass of water

Set: Used glasses for **Joan** and **Cliff**

Off stage: Ice bowl **(Stephen)**
Week-end case containing hair-dryer and white housecoat and turban
(Diane)

Personal: **Stephen:** watch, note
Sheila: engagement ring

LIGHTING PLOT

Property fittings required: Desk lamp, 2 table lamps, wall-brackets, electric fire
Interior. A lounge hall. The same scene throughout

ACT I, SCENE 1. Night

To open: Moonlight effect from windows and garden door

Cue 1	**Ray** switches on lights by garden door *Snap on all interior lighting*	(Page 1)
Cue 2	**Ray** kicks on electric fire *Bring up electric fire*	(Page 1)
Cue 3	**Stephen** turns off electric fire *Fade fire*	(Page 13)
Cue 4	**Norma** switches off lights *Snap off interior lighting and, a moment later, light on stairs*	(Page 14)

ACT I, SCENE 2 Morning

To open: Sunshine effect

No cues

ACT I, SCENE 3 Evening

To open: Effect of fading daylight. Fire on

Cue 5	As CURTAIN rises *Start slow fade to dusk*	(Page 18)
Cue 6	**Stephen** switches on lights *Snap on all interior lighting*	(Page 18)
Cue 7	**Stephen** switches off fire *Fade fire*	(Page 25)
Cue 8	**Stephen** switches off lights *Darkness in room except for moonshine*	(Page 25)
Cue 9	**Figure** moves into moonbeam *Flash of lightning*	(Page 25)

ACT II, SCENE 1 Night

To open: Room in darkness except for desk lamp

Cue 10	**Stephen** switches on lights *Snap on all interior lighting*	(Page 26)
Cue 11	**Stephen** switches off lights *Snap off all interior lighting except landing*	(Page 33)

ACT II, Scene 2   Night

To open: Room in darkness

Cue 12   **Stephen** switches on lights   (Page 33)
          Snap on all interior lighting

Cue 13   **Stephen** turns on fire   (Page 34)
          Bring up electric fire

Cue 14   **Diane** opens deed box   (Page 38)
          Snap off interior lighting and fire, bring up moonbeam

ACT II, Scene 3   Night

To open: Moonlight effect

Cue 15   **Sheila** backs away   (Page 38)
          Snap on all interior lighting, bring up electric fire

ACT II, Scene 4   Night

To open: All interior lighting on except desk lamp. Fire out.
            (Note: insert red bulb in desk lamp)

Cue 16   **Stephen** switches on desk lamp   (Page 49)
          Snap on desk lamp

Cue 17   **Stephen** switches off main lights   (Page 50)
          Snap off all interior lighting except desk lamp

Cue 18   **Tony** switches on main lights   (Page 51)
          Return to Cue 16 lighting

EFFECTS PLOT

ACT I

SCENE 1

Cue 1   As CURTAIN rises   **(Page 1)**
       Effect of rain, muted

Cue 2   **Sheila** closes door   **(Page 1)**
       Cut off rain effect

Cue 3   **Ray:** "Come on, love."   **(Page 2)**
       Telepone rings

Cue 4   **Norma** puts on record   **(Page 14)**
       Dramatic music, low volume

Cue 5   **Norma** turns off record player   **(Page 14)**
       Music off

SCENE 2

No cues

SCENE 3

Cue 6   **Stephen:** "Help yourself."   **(Page 22)**
       Thunder

Cue 7   **Figure** moves into moonbeam   **(Page 25)**
       Thunder

ACT II

SCENE 1

Cue 8   **Diane:** ". . . everyone, even himself."   **(Page 30)**
       Telephone rings

SCENE 2

Cue 9   **Diane:** "May I look?"   **(Page 37)**
       Telephone rings

SCENE 3

No cues

SCENE 4

Cue 10	**Stephen** puts on record *Soft music*	(Page 49)
Cue 11	**Tony** takes off record *Music off*	(Page 51)